Jacobson's

I miss it so!

THE STORY OF A MICHIGAN FASHION INSTITUTION

BRUCE ALLEN KOPYTEK

Charleston · London

THE
History
PRESS

Staircase with fountain and brick-lined escalator well, Jacobson's, Dearborn. Courtesy of the Ella Sharp Museum, Jackson, Michigan.

Published by The History Press
Charleston, SC 29403
www.historypress.net

Cover images are courtesy of the Ella Sharp Museum.
Images are courtesy of the author unless otherwise noted.

First published 2011
Second printing 2012
Third printing 2012

Manufactured in the United States

ISBN 978.1.60949.324.0

Library of Congress Cataloging-in-Publication Data

Kopytek, Bruce Allen.
Jacobson's : I miss it so / Bruce Allen Kopytek.
p. cm.
ISBN 978-1-60949-324-0
1. Jacobson's (Department store) 2. Department stores--United States--History. I. Title.
HF5465.U64J33 2011
381'.1410973--dc23
2011033111

To my dear mom, Bernadine, who liked shopping at Jacobson's, and for Carole, who helps me find my muse every day.

Contents

CONTENTS

Preface

A s a concept, the term "Atlantis" is able to take on several meanings. Greek philosopher Plato described Atlantis as an island given by Greek gods to Poseidon and eventually ruled by his son, Atlas. Plato's Atlantis sank beneath the waves, victim of a "terrible day of misfortune"—most likely a catastrophic earthquake. For most of us, the general, received understanding of Atlantis is that of a mythical utopia that no longer exists. The idea probably stems from English renaissance writer Francis Bacon's work *New Atlantis*, which described an island in the Pacific Ocean, named Bensalem, whose inhabitants were characterized by "generosity and enlightenment, dignity and splendour, piety and public spirit."

An inherent characteristic of Atlantis is a nostalgic yearning for what it represented. This longing for an ideal is intensified by the fact that it has disappeared and, consequently, is no longer attainable. The desire to find Atlantis, incredibly, exists despite the fact that in its pure sense, no one (at least living) has ever seen or experienced it.

There are, however, examples of Atlantis-like places that people do tangibly remember. The combined experience of the aristocracy in nineteenth-century Russia is one example. A whole class of people who spoke French in polite company, identified in the deepest way with the music of Tchaikovsky and were inspiration for the characters in Tolstoy's *Anna Karenina* was swept away in the cataclysm that engulfed Russia at the dawn of World War I. Over eighty years later, the name "Russia" was back and a market economy (of sorts) had replaced the brutal control of the communist yoke, but the society of merchants, aristocracy and academia—and the lifestyle with which they were familiar—was gone for good.

The American department store, as it existed in the last part of the nineteenth century and a large portion of the twentieth, is such an Atlantis in our own experience. When specifically remembered, it is sorely missed in an emotional way. The events that bound it to its patron's lives—the Christmas holiday, birthdays, weddings—still go along without its presence, but from time to time, a memory surfaces and the world of the past returns, if only for a fleeting moment. Atlantis seems to reappear above the churning waves; with it come memories of places and people who embodied the characteristics of Bacon's Bensalem. The tales that evoke these memories could entertainingly fill more volumes than just this one.

Merchandise acquired from one of these stores simply "had to" be good if it came from a place with cachet and fine repute. In Chicago, for example, it was, at one time, common to describe things as "that's Field's" if good and "that's not Field's" for the reverse, taking the name of the city's favorite store as synonymous with the best. By contrast, post-Atlantis, twenty-first-century American customers don't really care where an item comes from, and as long as they can get the brand name they covet, especially at a cheap price, it hardly matters to them that it was acquired from a big-box warehouse with a concrete floor and indifferent employees.

Each example of our department store Atlantis, while part of a larger group of deceptively similar organizations, was unique in its own place and time. Department stores gladly emphasized their *genus loci* in a great number of ways so that the stores themselves became integral parts of their communities. Department store restaurants, often named with local flair (Jacobson's well-regarded St. Clair Room in Grosse Pointe serves as an appropriate example, named, as it was, for the nearby body of water), also featured local specialties on their menus, driving home the relationship between even a small corner of a store to its host locality. Likewise, promotions, holiday celebrations and even department names could take on a local "accent," making the stores seem as inseparable from their communities as street names, rivers or other geographic and cultural aspects that served to define a locale.

The fact that thousands of citizens worked directly for this Atlantis, and even more clothed their families, furnished their homes and partook of social interaction in stores they respected, further solidified the bond between retail institution and place. One example of this connection stands out, if in a tragic way. In 1962, an Air France Boeing 707, carrying home the cream of Atlanta society from an art appreciation tour of Europe, crashed with the horrible loss of 130 lives. Rich's, Atlanta's most well-regarded department store, simultaneously sensed the feelings of fellow Atlantans and bound itself with their shock and grief by cancelling the next days' advertising and printing the words of the Twenty-third Psalm instead.

On the other hand, while the joyous, exuberant way in which these stores celebrated the Christmas holiday may have been economic in motivation, its effect on customers allowed the department stores to become a part of local family traditions. Repeated year after year, generation after generation, the traditions—and the environment in which they took place—became the basis for countless memories. These memories are what, if only momentarily, parts the waves that cover our long-disappeared Atlantis.

Jacobson's fits well into the Atlantis analogy. Once upon a time, Michigan had its own carriage-trade retailer, whose stores were firmly rooted in the downtown business districts of the state's thriving cities. Customers were welcomed into lavish, yet home-like, interiors and were addressed by name by a staff that, more often than not, wrote up sales slips atop antique reproduction desks. It was a place of good taste whose merchandise represented the finest selections, carefully edited to please customers it knew in an almost intimate way. While it began by serving women, it went from strength to strength in introducing children's wear, men's wear, decorative home goods and, finally, furniture to its offerings.

The store's growth and appearance on the Michigan scene were led by Nathan Rosenfeld, a true but unsung merchant prince who resolutely refused to consider anything that made "his" store seem less than the image of it in his own mind. Believing that the relationship between his business and the communities it served was of great importance, he became involved in projects he felt would help foster growth and prosperity, thereby helping Jacobson's expand. His common sense and perseverance of his personal ideals took a small but exclusive ladies' shop and made it, in a short time, into a highly respected chain of stores that were becoming identified with their locations across Michigan and, later, in Florida and various other places.

Like Atlantis, though, it is all gone now. Most of the more memorable Jacobson's stores are as unrecognizable as their communities in an economically devastated Michigan. It is hard to imagine today that a very common-looking medical clinic on an empty street of all-but-vacant shops was once a flagship of this retail empire. Or that the littered, youth-centered downtown of Ann Arbor, with its broken sidewalks, cheap coffee bars and convenience stores, was once the home of a plush, chandeliered store that was affectionately known as "Jake's"* to the minions who frequented the place in search of all that was stylish and good.

Unlike the ancient Atlantis, though, living people today still remember the store well and speak of it in high regard. Raise the subject of Jacobson's in any group of midwesterners or Floridians and the inevitable response will come: "Oh, Jake's! It's so sad that it's gone." Listen long enough and it becomes clear that the people who express these memories literally are the people of Atlantis.

Fortunately, our Atlantis only became submerged a decade or so ago. To be sure, the familiar logo or the handsomely conservative stores have disappeared from our streets, newspapers and, most importantly, from our celebrations and even our daily lives. Enough, though, remains to tell the tale of this beloved institution, tucked away in libraries on microfilm and in clipping files or stored in the vaults of one of Michigan's most important museums. In order to raise this Atlantis so that readers can get a glimpse into the experience that was Jacobson's, this book shall serve as a reconstruction of the organization, its facilities and its people, who will be shown to be brimming over with "generosity and enlightenment, dignity and splendour, piety and public spirit." Yet Jacobson's is sadly—and, it must be said, incomprehensibly—no longer with us.

---

* The diminutive term for Jacobson's is often encountered as "Jake's" or "Jac's." The former appellation will be used throughout this book.

Acknowledgements

I t is my most sincere desire to tell the story of Jacobson's with passion and accuracy and to show that the people associated with it were exemplary. I am grateful for the enthusiasm and magnanimity of those who were kind enough to assist me in this endeavor. Mark Rosenfeld generously came to the aid of a complete stranger and revealed a living connection to the management and ownership of Jacobson's. His dedication to the firm his father owned, and which he ultimately led, helped tell the story with a clarity that would have been impossible without his help and insight. Because of a chance call from Barbara Erbele of Jackson, I was able to discover the Jacobson's treasures located in the Ella Sharp Museum. There, Jim Zuleski generously spent hours guiding me through that institution's magnificent archives. Likewise, Jim Delaney welcomed me to his office and gave an insider's insight into Jacobson's. Pam Schauffler took a look at what I had done, offered her valuable perspective on the institution and put a final touch on my work. She became, for me, a fabulous guide to the world that was Jacobson's.

Elaine Coyne unselfishly assisted by putting me in contact with Jacobson's former employees and welcomed me into her home with gracious hospitality when I accepted her help. Lois Trost entertained me with her tales and, unbeknownst to her, gave me the title for this book. Others who have helped are Sigrid Wolf and James Sontag. Jan Curcio, Sharon Vick, Dolores Krosivek, Carol and Terry Markesino, Marikay Pigeon and Janet Heatley, of the Birmingham store, let me into the world they experienced at Jacobson's.

Likewise, Sandy Berardo, Cheryl Kutscher, Linda Salah, Sandra Meda, Lucille Howard and Cindy Brown, from the Grosse Pointe and Rochester stores, are worthy of sincere thanks for the enjoyable and enormously entertaining time they spent with me talking about Jacobson's.

Cheryl Chodun of WXYZ Channel 7 in Detroit helped give a well-known Detroit-area celebrity's idea of Jacobson's. I also thank author Michael Lisicky for helping me take my first few steps along a road he had traveled several times, producing books that served as an inspiration for this one.

Special thanks go to the kind and dedicated staff of the Ella Sharp Museum. In a similar way, much is owed to the staffs of the Jackson District Library, the Dearborn Public Library, the Baldwin Public Library of Birmingham, the Kalamazoo Public Library, the History Room at the East Grand Rapids Public Library and especially Chris Byron at the Grand Rapids Public Library for her enthusiasm. Isabelle Donnelly and the staff of the Grosse Pointe Historical Society were a tremendous asset to me as well. I am also grateful to the Washtenaw County Historical Society and the Jackson County Genealogical Society for their help.

My family, as always, deserves thanks for their encouragement and compassion while I concentrated on the task of writing about Jacobson's. Joan Kopytek discovered a connection to Jacobson's—her co-workers who were former Jake's alumni—and enriched the book beyond comprehension as a result. My goddaughter, Dr. Rachel Klamo, helped me keep a level head under pressure, and without a doubt, my wife, Carole, earned her angel's wings (or at least another pair of them) by being the helpful, understanding partner she has been through this process, including all of the hours it has kept me away from the time we love to share together.

Introduction

In April 2011, the Metropolitan Opera presented *Capriccio* for the first time in quite a few years. The 1942 opera by the Bavarian composer Richard Strauss is a nostalgic swan song created in war-ravaged Europe. Interestingly, it takes a question as its theme: in opera, what is more important, words or music? The work reaches its artistic climax when the cast itself decides to create an opera on the same idea, and the audience realizes that it is witnessing the very work about which the cast has sung. The heroine, a countess for whom the opera will be a birthday present, does not reveal, in the work's dénouement, whether she has chosen the words or music, represented by her two suitors, as paramount. Her butler announces, "Dinner is served!" and she merely exits the stage. She knows the answer, but the audience is left to wonder what it is.

It might seem strange to compare an opera to a department store. Yet the story of Jacobson's begs a similar question. What was primary, the stores themselves or the people who ran them? Or was it the customers? Was the store excellent simply by virtue of its owner, Nathan Rosenfeld, whose name should rest alongside those of Field, Wanamaker, Filene and Lazarus in the annals of American retailing?

Peeling back the foggy layers of time and revealing long-forgotten details, anecdotes and images provides a new insight into a great institution that has passed from the scene. A final answer to the question of what made Jacobson's great may be impossible to attain, just like the countess's unanswerable question in *Capriccio*.

Jim Delaney is administrator of human resources for the Jackson District Library, a role he fulfilled at Jacobson's as a vice-president since the 1970s. "There couldn't have been a better organization to work for," he says when reminiscing about Jake's. "When *Women's Wear Daily* wanted to do an article about us, they asked me, 'How do you do it? Your buyers have a 29,000-square-foot store in Winter Park, Florida, and a 200,000-square-foot one way up in Saginaw. How on earth can they buy the right merchandise for such disparate facilities?' The only answer I could give was that they didn't know how *not* to do it. They just did it. They were that good.

In his role at Jacobson's, he recalls that "the Company was as loyal to its employees as they were to it. If someone stayed three years, they were there for life!" Jim offers an example of this loyalty and mutual gratitude: "One day, in a meeting, we discussed granting an incentive of $10,000 to anyone who reached $1 million in sales. Over time, some of these salespeople achieved $2 million in sales. We talked about it, and management said, 'Cut them a check for $20,000.'"

Jim Delaney poses with a brass plaque that once graced the entrance of a Jacobson's store and is now a cherished souvenir of a great retail institution.

Quirky anecdotes about the store roll off his lips as if he were a master storyteller, and though his Jacobson's days are long past, he is as proud of his work for Jacobson's as he is of the bronze Jacobson's plaque he managed to rescue from one of the stores before it disappeared.

Mention the word "Jacobson's" in places like Grosse Pointe, Birmingham or Winter Park and the same comments will be heard again and again. "I really miss Jacobson's," former customers will say. They will go on to reminisce about that pair of shoes they got for a great price or about some special event they attended at Jake's. Some will remember eating in the hushed atmosphere of the restaurants, while others like to talk about local celebrities they saw perusing the offerings of this most cultured and luxurious store. It was famously said about Rich's, the great Atlanta department store, that "in all the world, no one speaks ill of Rich's." But the Jacobson name could be substituted and the statement would be equally true. It remains true to this day.

Patty Denton was a home furnishings buyer for Jacobson's. Now the owner of her own business, she offers her assessment of her experience with the store, saying, "I learned so much. Nathan Rosenfeld and Russ Fowler just naturally took people under their wings. I couldn't do what I am doing now if it weren't for the opportunities they gave me with Jacobson's."

For many years an administrative assistant in the office of Jacobson's Birmingham store, Elaine Coyne speaks about her experiences over a cup of coffee and some blueberry muffins she has just taken out of the oven. "The staff took such care to help the customers," she recalls, adding, "I liked my job; it was fun, and always interesting, too. I got to train people, and so I knew practically all of the employees. It was a special place; even answering the phone had to be done in a specific manner because we were representing Jacobson's." Her tone changes when she talks about the store's demise: "It was sad. People started to say, 'I can't find anything here anymore; they used to have such nice things.' When shoplifting started to grow, and they started playing rap music in the Miss J Shop, people just didn't like it." Then her eyes brighten up again. "Once, in 'the good old days,' I was looking for a dress for a special occasion after work. I didn't find what I wanted, and one of the girls asked me why I was leaving so soon. I described what I was searching for, and she said, 'Wait a minute, OK?' She came out of the stockroom with four dresses, and I had a hard time choosing which one to buy. Now that was Jacobson's! There was always something 'in the back,' and they were just great at helping a customer get exactly what they wanted."

Jim Zuleski worked for Jacobson's as a manager in Dearborn, Sarasota, East Lansing and, finally, Jackson before the company went out of business. He has found noble activity as the volunteer director of Collections and Exhibits in Jackson's Ella Sharp Museum. "My job at Jacobson's was always fascinating, and the store was a fine place to work," he reveals. "In Sarasota, all they had to do was open the doors, and the clientele would simply flow in, and sales would ring up, almost by themselves." Regarding Nathan Rosenfeld, Jim says simply, "Now, I loved the man, but please don't idolize him. He wouldn't have liked it. He wasn't perfect and could be really temperamental. People got fired all the time. But they knew Nathan well enough to come back the next day because no one stayed fired for long." (One buyer once responded to one of the firings by saying, "Look, I don't have time to be fired!")

Jim adds, "Nathan did have a heart of gold. For instance, we had one highly valued employee in the office who was plagued with a chronic illness. He barely showed up for work for six months. Someone asked Nathan, 'What do we do?' 'Well, pay the man!' Nathan said."

Pam Shauffler was a home economics teacher before she came to work for Jacobson's as secretary to the personnel director. "I had a career at Jacobson's which would not have been possible elsewhere," she asserts, "because Nathan Rosenfeld and Russ Fowler believed in people. I was given such freedom to find solutions to the challenges we faced." When she spent time at new stores for the purposes of recruiting and training new employees, she admits,

Jim Zuleski stands in the Jackson History Gallery of the Ella Sharp Museum with a photo of Nathan Rosenfeld, his former boss, beside him.

"I cried when my job was done because I had become so attached to the staff we put together." She rose to the position of vice-president of human resource development and is glad that she was able to visit the stores once or twice a year in order to keep in touch with the people who had become more than just employees and co-workers to her.

Cheryl Chodun, a well-known reporter with WXYZ Channel 7 in Detroit, is familiar to many in the region for her appearances on the television station's *Action News*. A loyal Jacobson's customer, she has pleasant memories of the time she spent shopping with her daughter at the Birmingham store. Cheryl enthusiastically adds, "I think about my shopping experiences at Jacobson's every time I drive by the corner where it once stood. They were always so friendly and helpful. It was, truly, one of the great stores."

Lois Trost worked as a manager in Jacobson's Grosse Pointe store for over twenty-five years. When her husband became ill, she had to go to work. So, on a warm day in 1970, she rode her bike to the store and took the job she was offered. Forty-one years later, Lois speaks of her time at Jacobson's as if it were a vacation in a well-loved resort. "I positively adored going to my job every day, and oh, brother! It was like a party with the best of friends. There was a lady named Louise, in the Custom Shop; I called her Wheezie. So she'd always walk down that ramp at the entrance to her department, the one we called 'Heartbreak Hill' because people tripped on it a lot, and call out to me, 'Wowis! How the hell are ya, kiddo!' Even after I retired, I became one of the 'call girls.' That meant I kept working part time whenever they needed me. Even though I wasn't there every day, it sure was nice to go back now and then."

She goes on to say, "I managed the toy department, and you know, Mr. Rosenfeld loved toys. Everybody was thrilled to death when we heard he was going to visit. It was the saddest thing in the world for us when he passed away." Wistfully, she recalls her years at the store and summarizes, "I don't have one regret. When I retired, it was me who owed Jacobson's; they didn't owe me a thing…and *I miss it so!*"

Ancient photo of the Reed City store. The words "Jacobson's Fancy Goods" can be seen painted on the store's front windows, while the interior is a far cry from what Jacobson's would later become. *Courtesy of the Ella Sharp Museum, Jackson, Michigan.*

Jacobson's Ladder

Starting in a small way, [Moses Jacobson] *applied practical business methods and his store prospered from the start.*
—Article in the Jackson Citizen-Patriot, 1928

Jacobson's earliest history is clouded in the distant past. This fact can be best illustrated by the images of a Jacobson's store, clearly from the nineteenth century, shown on page 24. For years, Jacobson's management in Jackson, Michigan, promoted the black-and-white photo as their original store in Reed City, Michigan, a small town in Osceola County, about seventy miles north of Grand Rapids. The firm went so far as to commission a line drawing of the building for use in annual reports and promotional material and later created a sketch of the store bedecked with Christmas wreaths and festoons for holiday advertisements.

Accepted by the store's management as a true representation of the retailer's early heritage, the images were put to intensive use, until it was brought to the attention of the Jackson headquarters in 1992 that the photograph was not of Jacobson's original store in Reed City but an image of Jacobson & Netzorg Company, a mercantile establishment in Greenville, Michigan, founded in 1873. Though it remains a mystery how Jacobson's came to acquire the Greenville photo, it is fair to deduce that the store, which had not been associated with Reed City for many years, simply saw the Jacobson name on it and made a false assumption that the large, elegant store had to be one if its own.

Photo of Jacobson & Netzorg, Greenville, Michigan, erroneously thought to be the Jackson-based retailer's original location. *Courtesy of Jim Delaney.*

Jacobson's origins in Reed City, arguably more humble than those of the eponymous Greenville establishment, are actually traceable with some acuity. The "real" Jacobson store was located at 102 East Upton Avenue, in the heart of this small lumber community in Michigan's northern forests. Its proprietor, Abraham Jacobson, was a Jewish immigrant to the United States from Poland—since the partitions of the eighteenth century—a part of the colossal Russian Empire. It is not known how or why he chose Reed City to begin his retailing venture, but records show that he married the former Esther Meister of Bay City, Michigan, and that the couple had three sons: Moses, William and Benjamin.

Abraham Jacobson threw open the doors to his "Fancy Goods" establishment in 1868 (although some sources claim 1869 or even 1870), and from the beginning, one of his strategies was to bring high-quality merchandise to the residents of Michigan's sparsely populated northland. Jacobson felt that women, in particular, would readily buy the same merchandise on display in New York's Fifth Avenue stores if they only had the chance. Reed City itself had only been settled in 1840, and received its charter as a village in 1872, but its population had grown to almost twenty-seven hundred by the last decade of the nineteenth century.

Jacobson's Ladder

At the very height of this growth, in 1892, Abraham passed away and left the business, still occupying its original 50- by 100-foot premises, to his sons. Moses Jacobson, who regularly traveled across Michigan with ten trunks full of merchandise for customers who were unable to visit the store, clearly witnessed the potential of the business while on these trips and longed to set up shop in a larger, more dynamic market than Reed City. Specifically, the prospects seemed bright, indeed, farther south, along the main line of what would become the Michigan Central Railroad connecting Detroit with Chicago via many of the Wolverine State's most prosperous cities: Ann Arbor, Jackson, Battle Creek and Kalamazoo.

Accordingly, in 1904, Moses moved to Jackson, Michigan, taking his brother William along with him. The youngest of Abraham's sons, Benjamin, remained in Reed City and ran the store there as a separate enterprise until the 1930s.

In Jackson, an announcement appeared in the *Jackson Citizen-Press* on January 14, 1904, stating that "Mr. M. I. Jacobson has purchased the stock of the Faulkner-Porter Co., 105 E. Main Street, and will continue the business...Mr. Jacobson has had considerable experience in this business [and] designs opening branch stores in adjoining cities, which will give him special facilities in purchasing."

Tellingly, by 1912, his store advertised:

> *We have figured it out this way: That every woman, to be perfectly satisfied with her outer apparel, must feel assured that she is properly and fashionably attired. That such a woman, clad in a Jacobson coat or suit is bound to be a pleased and satisfied customer and as such is the best recommendation we could desire for our garment department. Then you need not wonder, madam, why this store is so intent on pleasing you—it's one of our best business assets.*

The strategy must have worked well, for after several expansions at the original location, Jacobson began building a completely new facility in 1919, at 113 West Michigan Avenue in Jackson. On September 14, 1920, a grand opening advertisement for the new Jacobson's appeared in the *Jackson Citizen-Patriot*. The store was located in the Esther Jacobson Building, a structure purpose-built for the retailer and named for Moses's mother.

From the description provided by the newspaper, a mental picture of the store as an elegant emporium can be easily visualized:

Rivalling [sic] *the most exclusive metropolitan shops for beauty and artistic arrangement is the new Jacobson Shop, 115 West Michigan Avenue. The entire store is finished in ivory and light blue panels, with fittings, cases, and woodwork of cathedral brown oak. With the exception of the first floor, which is marble, the floors throughout the shop are covered with blue carpet with the Chippendale pattern outlined in black.*

The store was "thronged" with customers and had to remain open two hours later than normal "so that all may have the opportunity to see the beautiful displays of women's apparel."

By 1924, Moses had incorporated the business as Jacobson Stores, Inc., and his brother William operated the company's apparel department in Battle Creek, which was in space leased from a local department store. A second store was opened on Ann Arbor's Liberty Street, near the University of Michigan, in 1924. In 1926, another lease arrangement was concluded in Saginaw, Michigan, bringing the number of the company's outlets to four. When asked how it was possible to build his business so dramatically in such a short time, he answered simply, "I treat my customers right." It bears noting that Moses, as a member of the Rotary Club, Elks, Masons and Jackson Chamber of Commerce, was also familiar with society of the day. Described as a "master at personal trade," he was noted for contacting participants at Jackson's social events with suggestions about the latest fashions for them, which might be available in his store.

When Jacobson's was looking for information about its history, the store uncovered a tale about how Moses was always able to find some nice (and expensive) article for the small daughter of the store's landlord. When he showed her a costly beaver coat, which he said was a must for the finishing school she planned to attend, her father boiled with anger but was compelled to make the purchase. He later lightheartedly claimed that Jacobson's doting over his daughter was a way of reclaiming the rent he paid to the landlord.

When Moses Jacobson died of a heart attack in 1929, the *Citizen-Patriot* remembered him as "an outstanding example of the type of business man who makes his way to success through fair and honest dealing...and his success was not of the selfish kind. He could be counted on to support any enterprise for the public good." The operation of the store passed to his younger brother, William, who continued Moses's policies. But William had, by this time, developed heart disease and left the business in 1936 to live in a sanitarium. His son, Richard, reluctantly left law school to take over the family business, but his doing so was from a sense of duty, not from any inherent appreciation of the retail business. His heart was in the study of law.

It was no surprise, then, that in 1939, Jacobson's was put up for sale. Seemingly, the glory days under Moses Jacobson's leadership were in the store's past. It would not be long, however, before fate put another man of remarkable qualities into Jacobson's leadership role.

Illustration of the Esther Jacobson Building used for the grand opening of the store in 1920. *Courtesy of the Ella Sharp Museum, Jackson, Michigan.*

Nathan Rosenfeld (1903–1982, top) and Zola
Rosenfeld (1898–1961, bottom). *Courtesy of the Ella
Sharp Museum, Jackson, Michigan.*

Sovereign Nathan

There's a great future in retailing
for those of us who give our business a certain personality.
—*Nathan Rosenfeld*

With regard to Jacobson's, the year 1939 was marked by two undeniable facts: the store was run by a twenty-seven-year-old man who would have rather been in law school, and Nathan Rosenfeld, an executive at a store in Cincinnati, was interested in buying his own business so that he could be "the master of his own fate." The respective tracks of these two men intersected in Jackson, Michigan, near the corner of Michigan Avenue and Mechanic Street, in the fall of 1939, and in a sense, the modern Jacobson's came to be.

Rosenfeld, born in 1903, grew up in Philadelphia, to which his family had emigrated from Hungary. Showing intellectual and creative promise from an early age, he won a scholarship to the Philadelphia College of Art and later attended the University of Philadelphia's Wharton School of Business. He was one of a group of forward-looking young men in the world of retail of his day. Among his circle of friends was Stanley Marcus, of the Texas family who owned and operated Neiman-Marcus, one of the country's most renowned retail establishments. Marcus and others like Sidney Solomon, who went on to take the helm at Brooklyn's colossal Abraham and Straus, were destined to climb the corporate ladders of the nation's noted department stores. Nathan Rosenfeld, though, was a more individualistic creature who was interested in cutting his own path through the world.

Rosenfeld literally had retailing in his blood; as a youth, he helped operate his family's business and later held a prominent job at the Hecht Co. in Washington, D.C. He met his wife, the former Marjorie Leopold, after she crashed a wedding he was attending in the nation's capital. After a brief stint at an investment banking house, in the 1930s he found himself at Rollman & Sons, a long-established department store in Cincinnati, Ohio.

A memorable incident from this period not only illustrates his characteristic optimism but also his budding reputation as a "contrarian." At his instigation, Rollman's employees were treated to a lavish evening of dinner, drinks and music at the Queen City's most elegant hotel. Rosenfeld gave a speech in which he admonished the staff to avoid the despair that had gripped the country, rationalizing that the bottom had been reached and banks and businesses could no longer close but only reopen and grow as things got better. Even the hotel, which was generally too highbrow to have accepted a party for workers in the past, gladly participated because it was happy to have the patronage in lean times.

An able and valued executive, Rosenfeld, who turned down the presidency of Montgomery Ward & Company, was not satisfied, however, working for someone else. He was looking to buy a business in which he could apply the ideas that were literally brimming from his head and create a business that would be unique and result in a different kind of store—a store of his own.

A letter, dated September 17, 1939, from Nathan Rosenfeld to his older brother Zola, who at the time was merchandise manager at Allied Stores' Golden Rule in St. Paul, Minnesota, is key to understanding his motivation for buying a business and his aspirations as well. Writing as soon as he returned to Cincinnati from an exploratory visit to Jackson, he stated excitedly that "after having examined a score of propositions during the last several years, this [Jacobson's] is the first one which I liked without any reservations, liked so much that I am ready to tie myself up in any way necessary to make the purchase." He went on to explain that the Jacobson's he found was "without any reservation…the number one women's apparel and accessory store" in the cities in which it did business, explaining that the store was able to get high markups "not because management understands the technique of getting a high markup, but because these stores, established over a period of many years have won the right to get top lines exclusively…for most better manufacturers, it is just taken for granted that Jacobson's represents the right outlet for all of these three towns." At the time, the three Jacobson's stores were doing $300,000 in business annually. Rosenfeld himself would later say that he "was fortunate to buy a small business with a great reputation."

Rosenfeld went on to compare Jacobson's favorably with other stores in which he had worked and illuminated his findings regarding the three markets in which Jacobson's stores were located. After discussing the financial considerations of the purchase, he encouraged his brother to visit Jacobson's and consider going into business with him, adding that "with a limited investment, an acquisition such as Jacobson's is far more attractive than some big department store which is run down...where increases in sales mean endless demands for additional investment." After pointing out to Zola, who was "department-store minded," that "these are well-rounded-out women's specialty shops with real strength in shoes, millinery, hosiery, underwear and sportswear," he concluded, "I want you to consider this thing very carefully...even if you don't feel inclined to want to leave Allied immediately. I can run this business until such time as you are ready to join me; however, there would be plenty of work for both of us to do when you are ready."

One other "partner" was to become an integral part of the decision-making process and, indeed, was quietly present throughout the years of Nathan Rosenfeld's leadership at Jacobson's. His wife, Marjorie, whom he married in 1933, left memoirs from the time of Jacobson's 125th anniversary in 1993. In these invaluable recollections, she relates how the couple's two-year-old son Bobby was left with her parents, who were visiting Cincinnati, so that she and Nathan could go to Jackson to investigate Jacobson's. "We drove up to Jackson," she states, and "the beautiful trees and fall colors made a favorable impression upon us. The windows of the store were beautifully decorated with very fine merchandise. We learned later that the windows were very special because it was fall window week in Jackson. Nathan was suitably impressed with the stores, the figures and their potential."

Marjorie further indicates that Zola did make the trip, as asked by his brother, and that while he had "certain reservations and suggestions," he was generally agreeable to Nathan's proposal. She commented that, as always, Zola was the more cautious of the two brothers; his even temperament and thoughtful nature were complementary to Nathan's mercurial, effervescent spirit. Zola joined his brother as a partner in the business one year later, and the two brothers' different natures coexisted well.

Marjorie Rosenfeld stated that "knowing Nathan as I did, I knew that he would never be satisfied to run a business as small this one was," but "1939 was just a beginning. He and Zola had a vision for a greater future and plans for its long-term development." Enshrined in her notes about Jacobson's is the easy-to-recognize bond between her and her husband. Indeed, throughout the years, Marjorie remained at Nathan's side as he strived to attain his dreams and build Jacobson's into one of America's most respected specialty department stores.

Marjorie came to be seen as a fixture at Jacobson's and much more than just Nathan's partner in marriage. Pam Schauffler remembers her as "so much an integral part of Jacobson's." An able businesswoman, she handled the details of imports and customs and even penned company policy manuals. Many former Jacobson's

Marjorie Rosenfeld (1911–1995) in 1947. *Courtesy of Mark Rosenfeld.*

employees remember that on Nathan's walks through the store, he was often followed by Marjorie, with notebook and pen in hand. Surprisingly, though highly compatible, both of them were equally strong-willed; for instance, Marjorie was famous for insisting that the Terrace Room use her tuna noodle casserole recipe whenever the board of directors met.

Zola is remembered by many Jacobson's employees as the person who would show up and help "unruffle" feathers after Nathan's frequent, and occasionally stormy, store visits. A devout member of Temple Beth Israel in Jackson, he sponsored a series of lectures entitled "The Sunday Evening Hour," focusing on the common elements that bind major religious faith denominations. His death in 1961 robbed Jackson of a man who, as a member of both the Jackson Rotary Club and Planning Commission, was fond of saying that "we must not limit our plans to only those projects we will live to see." His son, Richard Z. Rosenfeld, served as Jacobson's legal counsel for many years.

On November 4, 1939, after negotiations with the Jacobson family, the sale of the store was completed, and Nathan Rosenfeld took the helm of the operation. An anecdote from his first day on the job reveals the nature of Rosenfeld's leadership and presages the way his nature would bear upon the future development of the small chain of three outlets. On Saturday, when he arrived at his office, he noticed that the store had advertised a major selling of furs to begin that day. Rosenfeld asked the bookkeeper, a Mrs. Price, to open the fur vaults so that the merchandise could be shown to customers when the store opened later that morning. A perplexed Mrs. Price told her new boss that Mr. Jacobson was the only person with the combination and that he had already left to go "up north" on vacation. In 1939, near the edge of Michigan's vast wilderness and well before the age of cellphones and e-mail, this meant that the combination was all but unavailable.

Earlier, Rosenfeld had been invited to join the Rotary Club to meet many of its members, one of whom was Harry Jackson, warden of the huge Jackson State Prison, the largest walled penitentiary in the world. Rosenfeld placed a call to the warden, explained his situation and asked if he could get some help. Soon, a prisoner, accompanied by guards, arrived and cracked the fur vault, thus saving the day. Rosenfeld himself rewarded the man with a meal in town before he was accompanied back to his lodgings behind the prison's forbidding masonry walls. The merchant often recalled this episode, an example of his own ingenuity and problem-solving skill, by saying that he "had no appreciation for outside consultants, except this one time" because "he had to go where the talent was!"

This little chestnut is much more than an amusing story. It is indicative of Rosenfeld's mixture of humor and inventiveness in putting his own business principles into action. His mind was full of ideas about how to make Jacobson's a store of ideals, and he had a knack for making a point in such a way that people didn't forget it.

Years earlier, when at the Hecht Co. in Washington, D.C., Rosenfeld had become convinced that the then-common practice of requiring floorwalkers to sign for every credit purchase was archaic and even counterproductive, so much so that signatures were being tossed off routinely, making them meaningless. When Rosenfeld proposed a streamlined approval procedure, he was rebuffed by the store's management, which did not see how foolish the practice had become. He was, though, finally able to convince management after he had salespeople solicit the floorwalkers' signatures on letters saying "I resign" without them even noticing what they were doing. The new approval process was soon in place as a result of this initiative, and the floorwalkers' time was freed up for them to do what they were hired to do: be of service to customers.

In a related incident at Jacobson's, Rosenfeld had a carton filled with garbage, wrapped and addressed to be sent to one of the chain's stores.

Clearly marked "Contents—Garbage," the package was duly delivered, and neither its contents nor its passage through the delivery process was ever questioned until it arrived at its destination and was opened. Rosenfeld was able to demonstrate to his employees how important it was for them to be alert and question practices that seemed to be suspect. In this way, he took an opportunity to show his employees that they were all important because they were all working to make Jacobson's the store it was meant to be.

In fact, Rosenfeld's attitude toward his employees was out of the ordinary. Aside from providing exceptional facilities for employees both at stores and at the company's headquarters in Jackson, he instituted policies aimed at getting—and keeping—the best employees he could find for Jacobson's. While he joked that the reason he refused to change Jacobson's policy of Sunday closings was that he didn't want to change the signs at the store's entrances, in reality he knew that his store's limited hours not only gave it cachet but also avoided myriad scheduling and staffing problems, and "better" salespeople would seek to work where they were guaranteed Sundays (and most evenings) off to spend with their families.

When he instituted Saturday closings in summer, for the sake of his employees, he had management ask salespeople if they thought they could sell as much in five days as in six. They answered in the affirmative, and the store, against all odds, experienced a healthy sales increase, despite decreased operating hours. The "family" atmosphere enjoyed by the company and its employees for years was a direct result of policies such as these. For many years, Jacobson's, no doubt as a result of its owner's ideals, had enviably low rates of employee turnover.

Rosenfeld's commitment to professional relationships is illustrated by a situation that occurred in his own office at the West Avenue Central Office and Distribution Center. He had a policy of keeping his office door open and answering his own phone. The idea seemed appropriate until he interrupted a conversation with one of his executives to take a call. When the executive complained that the interruption was rude, considering the seriousness of the topic at hand, Rosenfeld had a transfer button installed so that a secretary could take the calls when Rosenfeld was engaged. In fact, he encouraged his co-workers to challenge him from time to time so he could have the benefit of another voice against which to compare his own.

An inevitable result of good employment policies is that they attract good people, much as moths are attracted to light in the darkness. J. Russell Fowler was one such employee. A navy flag pilot who had flown Admiral Chester W. Nimitz during World War II, he met Rosenfeld while on leave in Jackson.

With a degree from Amherst College and experience in his father's drugstore and at Allied Stores' prominent Jordan Marsh Company in Boston, he joined Jacobson's at Rosenfeld's suggestion in 1945. Forming a team with the store's founder, the two complemented each other perfectly. Russ Fowler went on to join Jacobson's board of directors in 1955, was named vice-president in 1958 and became president of the company in 1966. Speaking of his experiences at the store, he said, "I've had the opportunity to develop an outstanding organization. Few people get such a chance."

The interiors of Jacobson's stores were, for many years, created in-house by the store's own unique design staff, headed by Keith Houck, another long-term employee. Working along with architects who devised plans for new stores and expanding the existing ones, Houck developed the "signature" look of the Jacobson environment throughout the 1970s. The consistency present in the company's stores was surely a result of Rosenfeld's relationship with employees like Houck; it was said that the stores were "Nathanized" after Rosenfeld inspected them and asserted his opinions about what he did and didn't like.

Display staff from various stores often worked as a single team to ready a new store for opening, creating stunning visual displays of merchandise to greet the customers streaming in on opening day. Working under the quiet and respectful leadership of Ted Matz, corporate visual supervisor, display managers from various stores would arrive and create magic and excitement as a unified team, despite the artistic freedom they were accustomed to at their home locations.

Jacobson's unique aura was characterized by store fixtures that resembled fine furniture, and indeed, the store's design team conceived its own fixtures, which were produced off-site by fine furniture manufacturers in Canada and the United States, thus avoiding a commercialized, mass-produced look and adding to the dignified residential tone the stores exuded. Another exclusive in this respect was the store's habit of displaying merchandise in the way it would be used, whether it be fashion apparel shown with coordinating accessories or home furnishings grouped as they would be in a customer's own residence. About Jacobson's visual presentation, *Women's Wear Daily* quoted an executive of "a major Detroit retailer" as saying, "It's what we aspire to. If we could be more like Jake's, we'd be happy. We just don't have what it takes."

Rosenfeld's ideals made a tangible impact on the cities in which he located stores. For many years, Jacobson's resisted putting stores in malls, believing, on a corporate level, that there wasn't a mall that lived up to the store's lofty standards. As a result, the store, at Rosenfeld's urging, paid great attention to the well-being of the downtown areas it inhabited. Rosenfeld worked tirelessly with Michigan cities to provide ample and convenient parking in their downtowns and was a pioneer in promoting the central cities as ideal places of business.

Key employees, such as Zola Rosenfeld and Russ Fowler, sat on the planning commission in Jackson, ensuring that the company's civic voice was heard prominently. In fact, store managers were expected to become active in their local communities, and it was store policy not to transfer them from town to town (common among other retailers) because Rosenfeld wanted them to become pillars in their places of business. Store employees who might aspire to become store managers were advised to take part in civic affairs as well. Another unfamiliar yet related fact is that the expressway signs pointing to Michigan's downtowns were first installed at Rosenfeld's suggestion.

Rosenfeld invested more than just a huge amount of time and effort into ensuring that these cities had ample, reasonably priced parking for customers in their central business districts. In some cases, Rosenfeld matched government funds dollar for dollar in order to make parking available, and in others, he bought municipal bonds and sold them at a discount to investment bankers, arranging financing so that the projects could go ahead.

In Jackson, when the company that operated the city's bus service went bankrupt, he organized business leaders to purchase used busses and operated a public transport system until the city was ready to take it over. Rosenfeld acted in spite of the fact that Jacobson's customers seldom rode the bus. It was done to safeguard the health of the downtown shopping district, of which Jacobson's was a part.

Once, Rosenfeld's civic-minded promotion of a comprehensive, well-financed and well-managed parking system for the city of Jackson was attacked as "self-serving" in the press by a local bank employee, ironically named Potter like the heartless character in the film *It's a Wonderful Life*. Rosenfeld's concern over this assault on his personal integrity caused him to contact the billionaire industrialist Norton Simon, whom he knew, to arrange backing to buy the bank whose employee had made the statement. With financing secured, he spoke to the bank's president, telling him, in no uncertain terms, that if the offending individual wasn't forced to retract the calumny, he would buy the bank and do so himself.

While this story may seem to indicate that Rosenfeld responded in a hostile manner, it was never in his nature to extract revenge from an adversary. His action, his son Mark recalls, was the response of a deeply principled man whose integrity was called into question without any real justification.

The constant expansion and improvement in the company's stores was a result of yet another of Rosenfeld's deeply held ideals. "A business is like a cathedral, it should never be finished," he opined and backed it up with action, believing that it was more advantageous for Jacobson's to own its stores than to rent them. Though unheard of in the retail business, ownership of major facilities allowed Rosenfeld to reinvest tax savings gained by depreciation, and he often said that "depreciation is a physical fact, not an accounting fiction." As a result, Jacobson's stores perpetually grew and expanded, while maintaining the fresh, elegant character that well-heeled customers came to appreciate. To illustrate, Rosenfeld said, "The place of doing business is a retailer's stock in trade" and that "if we [businessmen and landlords] take depreciation on real estate and think it's a profit, we're crazy. Unless we reinvest money from depreciation, we have nothing but blight to show."

Like his commitment to his employees, and to the communities where his stores did business, Rosenfeld also considered his relationship with his customers as key to Jacobson's success. Famously, he described his rapport with customers, saying:

> If we don't represent the interests of the customer, who will? We only do the things that we think our customers will like and buy the things that we are proud to sell them. We are interested in holding onto their confidence over the years, rather than sell them the things that may be opportunistic for us to sell at the moment, because there may be a great demand for the item or an unnatural demand created by a manufacturer who is only interested in the immediate market possibilities for his product.

It was, and still is, common practice for manufacturers to prepare "packages" of merchandise for individual stores, the idea being that the manufacturer takes responsibility for the stores' needs. Saying that "we are not a vending machine for the manufacturer," Rosenfeld urged Jacobson's buyers to reject this approach and act as purchasing agents for the store's customers. Jacobson's merchandise was carefully edited from manufacturers' offerings with its own diverse individual markets in mind. This meant that buyers selected from assortments presented to them with intimate knowledge of the Jacobson's customer, and in some cases, such as the store's high-end designer business, items were even chosen based on the needs of individual customers with whom buyers were familiar.

Rosenfeld was proud of the fact that Jacobson's buyers were considered tough; it was done on behalf of the customer and helped build the store's credibility. He refused to allow comparative pricing, whereby an item was advertised as "regularly $50, now $29.95," because it indicated that the store was promoting an item that wasn't worth the $50.00 to begin with. Looking back at many years of Jacobson's advertising, it is not possible to find full-page sale ads, gimmicks or promotions because Rosenfeld felt such things eroded the store's credibility. Coupons were likewise considered taboo because it was unfair to a customer who, by simple fact of circumstance, didn't have one. The wisdom of these policies was not only borne out by Jacobson's longevity and growth but also by one succinct example. When the Detroit area endured a major newspaper strike in the 1960s, retail sales suffered, but Jacobson's enjoyed an increase in business. Rosenfeld built up a clientele that came not just *to* but *for* Jacobson's, where they got service, quality and a fair price—not just a price and price alone.

Rosenfeld's sense of humor was infamous. Among many tales of his idiosyncrasies, those about his gag products have attained legendary status. He presented employees with ties patterned with the letters Y C D B S O Y A ("You Can't Do Business Sitting On Your Assets") as a motivational gag. They promptly became bestsellers in the stores. Despising "buzz words," he ordered cocktail glasses printed with them, including a "bottom line" to signal the need for a refill. When it was discovered that the word "psychographics" was misspelled on the glasses, omitting the first "h," he quipped, "Forget about it. That's how it should be spelled!"

When counting as many as eight separate tags hanging on a dress button by a particular manufacturer, Rosenfeld had vice-president of advertising William Melms create an award certificate for vendors who burdened their merchandise with so much superfluous material. Called the "Hangtag Award," it was sent out to manufacturers with a letter from Rosenfeld himself asking if "perhaps there should be more than eight tags" and thanking the firm for its "contribution to the government's full-employment policy." A spurious contest among employees to see who could remove the most "unnecessary tags and return them to our marking room, whereupon we give them credit as if turning in trading stamps" was also mentioned in the tongue-in-cheek correspondence.

The most outrageous examples of his wit were most certainly the fake men's colognes he devised, due to his distaste for men's fragrances, in spite of the fact that Jacobson's sold millions of dollars worth of them. "Essence of Stale Cigars" and "Essence of Putting Green" were two of

Sovereign Nathan

Pencil sketch done by an unknown but obviously grateful employee on the occasion of Nathan Rosenfeld's fortieth anniversary with Jacobson's. The image uniquely conveys his legendary sense of humor. *Courtesy of the Ella Sharp Museum, Jackson, Michigan.*

the more mild ones, while "MANURIQUE" showed the devilish side of his caprice. He even issued a jocular memo asking for ideas on how the store could capitalize on the "streaking" craze of the 1970s, facetiously predicting that the lack of clothing in public could hurt Jacobson's profit picture if it became too fashionable.

In 1939, however, this all remained locked in Nathan Rosenfeld's head; he was just another new business owner in a small but prosperous town called Jackson. What would transpire, though, is surely the stuff of retail legend.

Early photo of Jacobson's interior after Nathan Rosenfeld acquired the store. Clearly visible are level changes between the various buildings and archways cut through bearing walls, but the street floor was elegant and service-oriented, in spite of cramped quarters. *Courtesy of the Ella Sharp Museum, Jackson, Michigan.*

You Don't Know Jackson

The old established center of a retail district of a town represented an evolution.
The weakness in most malls is that they try to create an instant success.
—Nathan Rosenfeld

When Nathan Rosenfeld took control of Jacobson's, it was still located in the Esther Jacobson Building, built by his predecessor, Moses Jacobson, in 1920. Downtown Jackson was a thriving retail district that drew patrons from miles around. It was said at the time that residents of the state capital, Lansing, some forty miles to the north, preferred shopping in Jackson, which had a better-developed central business district.

Jacobson's was but one major retailer competing for business in Jackson, then known as the Rose City. Fashionistas of the day frequented the Elaine Shop and the Margaret Mary Shop on Michigan Avenue, but downtown Jackson's "big" department store was the L.H. Field Co., incorporated in 1891. Field's founder, Leonard H. Field, was a cousin of Marshall Field, and in many ways, his store was to Jackson what the great State Street emporium bearing his cousin's name was to Chicago. In the early 1950s, Field's expanded and remodeled its neo-Gothic building and sheathed it in aluminum panels, giving it a modern look. Field's Rose Room was a popular place for Jackson shoppers to meet, eat and be seen.

Jacobson's store at 113 Michigan Avenue began to expand shortly after the sale to Rosenfeld. By 1945, the Palmer-Reynold and Lockhart Buildings were acquired to the east of the Esther Jacobson Building. Archways were

Jackson's large L.H. Field department store. Under the modern, 1950s façade was an old neo-Gothic building, but Field's was a respected retailer that dominated downtown Jackson for many years. *Courtesy of the Ella Sharp Museum, Jackson, Michigan.*

cut into the walls between the structures in order to expand and connect the sales floors. Additional floors were added to the two acquisitions, but the building lacked unity from outside and within.

By the end of the decade, another adjacent structure known as the Farnham Building was added to the flagship store. With this addition, the ground floor was sheathed in polished stone, and a new central entrance was installed, with the company's understated new logo painted in gold on the transom over the doors. With the growth of Jacobson's and its expansion into new merchandise lines, more office space was acquired, first across the alley and later on the second and third floors of the Webb Building on Mechanic Street, which was linked by a bridge to the burgeoning Jacobson's complex.

Aside from the increase in space, further evidence of Rosenfeld's desire to create a full-line specialty department store was conveyed during this time by the opening of a shop for home decorative items. In 1953, Jacobson's opened a completely new men's shop at 257 West Michigan, farther west down Jackson's main retail street and on the other side of Field's.

In 1955, perhaps inspired by the radical remodeling of Field's, Jacobson's united its conglomeration of disparate buildings behind an elegant modern façade of red granite at the street floor and light porcelain panels above. With the store's long-established ladies' wear shops, children's apparel and

Jacobson's grew through the first half of 1940s by leasing adjacent properties. *Courtesy of the Ella Sharp Museum, Jackson, Michigan.*

home furnishings, presented under the same roof, it would seem that the Jackson store had achieved its desired position as a flagship location for the enterprise. J. Russell Fowler, however, when recalling his years at 113 West Michigan, stated, "It was really a pain. I was glad we got out of there when we got out of there!" Aside from the compromises of presenting merchandise in cobbled-together buildings, the top-floor offices, spread out behind the new façade, were unbearably hot in the summer, prompting Rosenfeld to jokingly declare a "four-day-or-less" per week employment policy due to absenteeism in the sweltering weather.

In 1955, Jacobson's acquired a modern image by installing porcelain panels over its collection of buildings, which by that time had expanded to include the Farnham building to the east of its main store. *Courtesy of the Ella Sharp Museum, Jackson, Michigan.*

Jacobson's expanded into the men's wear market in 1953, but the store was located one block west of the main store, near a site that would later house the 1961 Jackson store. *Courtesy of the Ella Sharp Museum, Jackson, Michigan.*

In the late 1950s, the first steps were taken to replace the Jackson store with something new, modern and purpose-built. Negotiations to extend the leases on the existing buildings were not satisfactory, so Rosenfeld went about acquiring property around the 1953 men's shop. His goal was to acquire enough property to build a representative Jacobson's in downtown Jackson, stretching from a new front on Michigan Avenue all the way back to Cortland street, where ample surface parking was available for customers. The existing Dowsett Building on Cortland Street was acquired to house the young men's Mr. "J" Shop, the Cortland Room restaurant and a beauty salon on the second floor.

After the ribbon was cut on August 21, 1961, by Jackson mayor Bernie Magiera, over five thousand Jacksonians turned out to tour the fifty-three-thousand-square-foot facility with its spacious floors, colorful displays and state-of-the-art lighting. Advertised as the "fashion center of the future, now in Jackson," the new store formally opened for business on the next day. One notable feature of the planning for the complex was the partially covered through-block passageway, which not only served the Jacobson store but also allowed Michigan Avenue shoppers comfortable access to parking, one of Rosenfeld's goals—a veritable "gift" to the city.

Jacobson's 1961 store gave it a fresh, modern presence on Michigan Avenue and a partially covered passageway from the shopping street to parking in the rear. The bright, contemporary interior was a notable improvement over its previous location and combined all merchandise categories under one roof. *Courtesy of the Ella Sharp Museum, Jackson, Michigan.*

Jacobson's renovated the downtown Jackson Sears store into a Store for the Home after it purchased Daly Brothers furniture of Dearborn, Michigan. *Courtesy of the Ella Sharp Museum, Jackson, Michigan.*

When Jacobson's expanded into the furniture and floor coverings markets, it acquired the former downtown Sears store on the corner of Cortland and Blackstone Streets. In 1969, after a renovation, which renewed the interior and gave the building a "new" Colonial-style exterior, Jacobson's was able to offer all of its home furnishings merchandise in one location, along with a brand-new furniture "Galleria." The new Store for the Home allowed departments in the main store to expand into space previously dedicated to china, gifts and linens, which had relocated to the new building.

In the ensuing years, the store was renewed from time to time, as was Jacobson's policy. The modern interior gave way in the early 1970s to a richer, more traditional style typical of Jacobson's stores of the era, and its signature designer boutiques were installed among its other fashion offerings. In spite of the opening of Westwood Mall in Jackson in the early 1970s, Jacobson's continued to fulfill its role not just as an anchor but also as a destination itself for shoppers and even local office workers, for whom the Cortland Room restaurant was a popular lunchtime rendezvous.

Jacobson's was different from many of America's notable department stores because it didn't have one "flagship," multistory department store with smaller branches radiating from it. Each of the stores was considered by Nathan Rosenfeld to be a "neighborhood store," and while they varied widely in size, they operated as a collection of equals within the organization. In fact, credit card billing was handled at the local level as the store grew, in order to reinforce the community focus of the individual stores. Initially, management was housed in the aforementioned offices on the top floors of the Esther Jacobson Building. When the store building proved inadequate to accommodate Jacobson's growing administrative needs, and more space was leased across the alley, buyers were moved away from the store building proper.

Rosenfeld saw a benefit to this arrangement because buyers were not specifically attached to the Jackson store alone. The benefit was that the buyers themselves had to consider each of the store's outlets individually, but equally, if the company was to most effectively serve customers across Michigan.

Russ Fowler also assessed the office situation and began, with the help of the store's buyers, developing the concept of a central office combining distribution, buying and administrative functions at one location. Rosenfeld, however, needed to be convinced. He was dead set against the idea of warehousing fashion merchandise. When presented with the facts that centralized buying and distribution could actually help buyers make better decisions for Jacobson's, and save money in the process, he was compelled to break his own rule and ordered the development of the complex in time for his tenth anniversary at Jacobson's in 1949.

It was, in fact, the first central distribution facility developed to handle fashion merchandise outside New York City. Later, Fowler remarked that "the system greatly contributed to the growth of Jacobson's. From that point on, Macy's, Sears, Federated and others visited to look at our operation."

The facility, which opened in November 1949 at 1200 West Avenue, north of Jackson, was genuinely out in the cornfields at the time. Along with offices for company management, it provided space for administrative functions such as accounting, advertising and store planning and the merchandising operations of buying, receiving, marketing and distribution. Increased quality control for Jacobson's was a byproduct of the innovative central distribution system. "CD" thus became the nickname for Jacobson's head office.

The new building was enthusiastically occupied through the winter months of 1950, but as the weather grew warmer, an olfactory problem surfaced. The farmer next door boarded his horses on the adjacent property, and since the building did not have air conditioning, the stench made working conditions unpleasant. Rosenfeld, as ever, was quick to find a solution. He offered the farmer a new car if he would move the

Jacobson's West Avenue corporate office and central distribution, pictured in the 1960s; Nathan Rosenfeld's office and its "open door" are clearly visible. *Courtesy of the Ella Sharp Museum, Jackson, Michigan.*

Nathan Rosenfeld (left) and vice-president of advertising William Melms (right) welcome bridal consultant Vivian Colson and her daughters to an open house celebrating one of central distribution's frequent expansions. *Courtesy of the Ella Sharp Museum, Jackson, Michigan.*

horses to another one of his properties. The farmer accepted the offer and was so enamored by the generosity of Jacobson's that he became an unofficial—and, at times, unappreciated—twenty-four-hour watchman for the CD, calling executives at any hour of the day or night about the slightest suspicious activity. In time, the CD had to be expanded, and the farmer's property was purchased, putting an end to the neighbor problem.

The location outside town also necessitated a dining facility, which eventually moved to the second floor and was named the Terrace Room during one of the building's many expansions. Rosenfeld decided that the CD needed a motto and had it translated into Latin by a local high school teacher: *Si labor faciendus est, hic est bonus locus.* Meaning "If you have to work, this is a good place," the motto appeared on the walls and on blue condiment packages in the dining room throughout the store's lifetime.

When computerization came to the CD, Rosenfeld frequently showed visitors the installation, claiming that the store also had a hugely expensive backup system in case of a computer shutdown. By this, he meant the abacus he had acquired and hung on the wall in the computer room, in reality showing that his business was rooted in common sense, as well as more than just a bit of humor.

When speaking of Jacobson's headquarters, it is also worth mentioning the concept, developed by Rosenfeld, of the "Million Dollar Round Table." In essence, Rosenfeld had pins made and issued them to any buyer whose merchandise markdowns had reached $1 million. While seeming to rib the buyers for their mistakes, Rosenfeld explained that the reward was for taking risks, and in spite of their mistakes, they were able to learn from them and go on to be better buyers. The pins were distributed at Monday morning meetings around a conference table, the round shape of which was dictated by Rosenfeld, so that no one was located at the head and all participants could feel free to speak their minds about what was going on at the store.

It was Rosenfeld's turn to be teased when a friend absconded with his own pin and had a diamond mounted on it. When it was returned to Rosenfeld, he was told that he deserved the jewel because if Jacobson's had buyers who took a million in markdowns, Rosenfeld himself would have to have been responsible for ten times that at least!

The CD was expanded again and again as Jacobson's grew. In 1982, a similar facility was located in Winter Park, Florida, to serve the growing number of stores in that state. The original CD was no longer out in the country but surrounded by a typical suburban "strip" environment by the late 1980s, when it was replaced by a completely new headquarters on Sargent Road, overlooking Brills Lake, in 1988.

Neither Jacobson's history nor its future growth remained within the boundaries of the city of Jackson. When Nathan Rosenfeld purchased the business, it was already a chain of three stores, and the transformation of these stores was soon undertaken by the firm under its energetic leader.

Like most Jacobson's stores, the Ann Arbor store changed recognizably over the years. A major remodeling in 1969 included a large parking deck over part of the building, and it eventually received a new façade of richly-detailed brickwork. *Courtesy of the Ella Sharp Museum, Jackson, Michigan.*

A [Squared]*

See how beautiful a store can be! One magnificent department after another reflecting the fashion awareness of today.
—Jacobson's advertisement, Ann Arbor News, 1969

One of the original Jacobson's stores, inherited when Nathan Rosenfeld purchased the chain, was located at 612 Liberty Street in downtown Ann Arbor, virtually across the street from the University of Michigan. In his 1939 letter to Zola, he mentions that the store sales dropped off during the summer, not surprising given that Ann Arbor at the time had a population of twenty-eight thousand, which was almost doubled during the school year. Nonetheless, he went on to say that he and Marjorie found the town "most attractive."

Like most Jacobson's stores, the Ann Arbor unit grew piecemeal by acquisition and expansion. The store first acquired the Sager-Adams Building on Liberty Street and eventually moved into the Ann Arbor Press and University Music School buildings along Maynard Street. Jacobson's competitors, Goodyear's and Kline's, were located on the city's traditional downtown strip, Main Street, but the Liberty Street location carried its own cachet, around the block from a Saks Fifth Avenue college store and an arcade filled with upper-class shops.

The store, originally a small women's shop, continued to grow bit by bit, expanding to fill a major downtown block and by converting second-floor

---

* University of Michigan academic speak for Ann Arbor, A²

A 1930s view of Jacobson's on Liberty Street. Like many of the company's stores, it would not remain recognizable as this for very long. *Courtesy of the Ella Sharp Museum, Jackson, Michigan.*

apartments to sales space and excavating under existing properties to expand the store's lower level.

A major remodel in 1941 was heralded in the *Ann Arbor News*, which reported that "a wide-eyed public left the store feeling that it had seen the last word in ultramodern store design" and that "Ann Arbor's sophisticated and unsophisticated sets inspected the store from beautiful façade to ultra modern fitting rooms." Another major addition in 1955 brought the store up to fifty-seven thousand square feet.

In the midst of all of the construction and renovation, a competing dress shop remained an obstacle on Jacobson's side of Liberty Street. Nathan Rosenfeld was reluctant to purchase the store because it would decrease competition in the area, and when a fire made a vacant piece of property available across the street, Rosenfeld acquired it, built a building and leased the space to the shop. In this way, he was able to get space for Jacobson's expansion needs but also enhanced the retail environment in which the store operated.

The sophisticated 1941 interior delighted the press and customers. The "Circle Room," visible in the rear, was where the very best fashions on offer were sold. *Courtesy of the Ella Sharp Museum, Jackson, Michigan.*

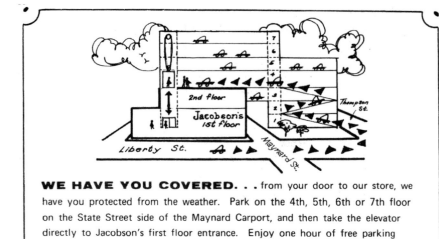

WE HAVE YOU COVERED. . . from your door to our store, we have you protected from the weather. Park on the 4th, 5th, 6th or 7th floor on the State Street side of the Maynard Carport, and then take the elevator directly to Jacobson's first floor entrance. Enjoy one hour of free parking while you shop at Jacobson's. We will be pleased to validate your parking ticket.

Jacobson's touted the ease of parking in the garage adjacent to its store. Such ads were sent directly to account-holders. *Courtesy of the Ella Sharp Museum, Jackson, Michigan.*

The main entrance to the expanded store was under the Maynard Street parking deck. *Courtesy of the Ella Sharp Museum, Jackson, Michigan.*

A [Squared]

Early in his ownership of the store, Rosenfeld paid a visit and proclaimed the office area too large, ordering parts of it converted into sales space. After his wishes were carried out, he came again, expecting to find a particular employee. Rosenfeld was told that her desk had been moved to the receiving room as a result of his reconfiguration plan. Upset that the employee had to work in unpleasant conditions, he immediately had her office restored to her. The incident was a notable illustration of the regard in which the store held its employees.

In fact, Ann Arbor in the early 1970s was the scene of another episode that serves well to illuminate the bond between Jacobson's and its staff. The store found itself in a crisis because a University of Michigan graduate student, originally from Britain, initiated a drive to organize Jacobson's employees into a union as a basis for his master's thesis. Store executives bent over backward to thwart the attempt, which they saw as an outside attack on the "family" atmosphere they had tried to maintain at Jacobson's. Managers met one morning with employees to "talk out" the situation, and when the meeting extended past the store's opening time, executives themselves went to the doors and apologized to customers who wished to come in and shop, saying, "We are sorry, but the store has an emergency and can not open until later, when we hope you will be able come back." Turning to the employees, they reiterated Nathan Rosenfeld's belief that "as important as our customers are, there isn't a single customer as important as our employees, and we'll stay here all day to work it out if necessary."

Eventually, Jacobson's won the employees' vote hands-down, and the organization attempt fizzled. The integrity of the business under Nathan Rosenfeld was again illustrated when, after this incident, he oversaw the creation of new corporate positions meant to ensure consistent standards of fair employee treatment and training in all stores.

In 1969, a major construction project more than doubled the Ann Arbor store to 115,000 square feet and expanded its offerings to include home furnishings. The five disparate properties that Jacobson's had acquired through the years were consolidated into one, forming a suave and opulent downtown anchor worthy of the Jacobson's name. Consistent with Rosenfeld's belief that convenient and ample parking was key to healthy central business districts, the store was integrated with a new civic parking deck on Maynard Street, above the new part of the store. Jacobson's leased the support columns for the deck, which penetrated the store, to the city for a token fee, prompting Rosenfeld to jest that it was "like leasing the holes in Swiss cheese!"

In its newly expanded form, the store surely outshone its predecessor of twenty-eight years earlier; Jacobson's own ads invited customers to "see how beautiful a store can be!" Opening the heavy wooden doors, which formed a new entrance under the parking deck, customers entered a haven of calm and elegance, a tangible contrast to the brash college-town atmosphere outside.

At the same time, Jacobson's, which had in the previous year purchased Daly Brothers Furniture in Dearborn, took control of Martin Haller Interiors, a respected Ann Arbor home furnishings retailer operated by Dick Manville, a former professional baseball player who played for the Chicago Cubs and the Boston (now Atlanta) Braves. The purchase allowed Jacobson's to integrate a fine interior design studio into its home furnishings offerings, and Manvillle stayed on for a while as vice-president of the division.

In the early 1980s, the store was further remodeled and given a more traditional brick exterior. Two additional properties on State Street, almost across from the University of Michigan's quadrangle, first housed the store's

The acquisition of two existing properties extended the store onto State Street. These buildings were eventually connected to the main store. *Courtesy of the Ella Sharp Museum, Jackson, Michigan.*

A [Squared]

Mr. "J" Shop and had to be accessed across an open alley, but in 1983, the Furniture Galleria and interior design studios were relocated there, and the alley was enclosed for a better transition from the main store.

Ann Arbor remained one of Jacobson's most popular stores for many years, but as time went by, deteriorating conditions in Ann Arbor's downtown, especially with regard to parking, were to change the store's relationship with the city dramatically.

The Trump Block, the location of Jacobson's first Battle Creek store. The street floor was dwarfed by the adjacent Kresge store. The stair leading to the upper floors is visible at the back, on the left. *Courtesy of the Ella Sharp Museum, Jackson, Michigan.*

Cereal Number

*It will greatly hurt downtown Battle Creek. Now I feel I won't be going
downtown as much as I did in the past.*
*—Anonymous customer responding to a survey about Jacobson's 1980 proposal
to close the Battle Creek store*

Nathan Rosenfeld's purchase of Jacobson's included an early branch
store in Battle Creek, Michigan, the self-proclaimed "Cereal Capital
of the World." It was opened in 1937 by William Jacobson, in an unusual,
somewhat compromised location known as the Trump Block in downtown
Battle Creek, at 33 West Michigan Avenue. The branch had a narrow,
sixteen-foot-wide space on the street floor, with elevator and stair access in
the back to two larger floors over the local Kresge store next door. After
Rosenfeld took possession of the store, he had severe reservations about the
safety of the upper floors and their fire escape route. Expressing his concerns
to the landlord, he threatened to withdraw rent unless the building was made
safe for his employees and customers.

The Battle Creek store was the first in the Jacobson's chain to broaden
the store's merchandise mix, due to an employee whose familiarity with
the children's wear market made it possible to begin buying operations in
that area. After proving successful in Battle Creek, children's shops were
opened in other Jacobson's stores. Nathan Rosenfeld often remarked that
the children's wear market, though a difficult one for many retailers, had a
twofold benefit to the store. Mothers, bringing children into Jacobson's, could
see all the latest on offer for themselves as well, and as the children grew,

The Post Building was Jacobson's home in Battle Creek from 1951. *Courtesy of the Ella Sharp Museum, Jackson, Michigan.*

they became potential Jacobson's customers. Rosenfeld proudly described the store's children's shops as "where we grow our customers."

For a long time, management wanted to relocate the store. A prime retail building in Battle Creek was to be sold at auction, which Nathan Rosenfeld attended personally, in order to make a deal. However, he returned to Jackson grumbling that he "never had a chance" once the super-wealthy industrialist and founding partner of General Motors, C.S. Mott, showed up, brandishing not one, but three checkbooks, which he used to pay for the building. Mott's charitable foundation owned a number of department stores in Michigan, notably Smith-Bridgman of Flint, Knapp's of Lansing and Robinson's of Battle Creek, and the coveted site became the home of the latter organization.

Undaunted, in 1951, Rosenfeld had the store moved to the corner of Michigan Avenue and McCamly Street, in the half-century-old Post Building, built by cereal magnate Cyrus W. Post. During the renovation of the building, Rosenfeld noticed a worker who was patching concrete on an upper floor. The worker had a small Scottie on the job with him that nipped at Rosenfeld's ankles whenever he got close to the wet cement. He was amused by the dog owner's revelation that the pup was trained to keep anyone away from the uncured concrete, and as long as he stayed clear of it, he had nothing to fear. Rosenfeld was so taken by the incident that he often retold it in order to describe what he considered the "excellent training" Jacobson's would do well to emulate.

Another legendary story that originated in the Battle Creek store was often repeated by Rosenfeld as an indication of Jacobson's status as a customer service leader. A robber entered the store and approached a saleslady by the name of

Cereal Number

Thelma Quartermaine, who happened to be engaged with a customer at one of the counters. He attempted to interrupt their conversation with the words "This is a holdup!" but the employee, focused on her patron, didn't even realize what he had said and retorted, "Can't you see I am busy with a customer?" This broke the would-be criminal's will. Whether he robbed another business after the rebuff at Jacobson's is not recorded, but Rosenfeld said of the incident, "Doesn't that just show you the dedication of our salespeople?"

The Battle Creek store, though profitable, presented a number of strategic problems for Jacobson's. Its policy of being a downtown anchor in the cities in which it operated meant that the provision for parking was of utmost importance. Rosenfeld personally became involved in land purchases and negotiations for parking that would benefit not only his store in Battle Creek but also the whole downtown area, one of the weakest shopping districts in which the company was located. In his initial letter to Zola, Rosenfeld mentioned that Battle Creek didn't have "a decent department store in the city," in spite of its population of fifty thousand. Convinced, however, that Battle Creek held great potential for Jacobson's, Rosenfeld was thwarted again and again in attempts to build a bigger store in the city.

A pedestrian mall along Michigan Avenue, built in the wake of a similar project in nearby Kalamazoo, was not only unsuccessful due to poor execution and planning but also seriously compromised traffic and access to the store, as did a maze of railroad tracks in the center of the city. Nathan Rosenfeld, when speaking to colleagues about the Battle Creek store, disparagingly said that it was a victim of "mall practices" and even took executives on a convoluted car ride through the city to prove how difficult it was for customers to come downtown to shop given the status quo in Battle Creek's central business district.

In June 1980, Jacobson's announced that the store would close, but Rosenfeld later rescinded the decision when the city and the store's landlord offered help to keep it downtown by searching for solutions to the district's problems. Two years later, though, citing a lack of progress in replacing the thirty-three-thousand-square-foot store, Rosenfeld said, "We have been unable to reconcile ourselves to operating a facility which is so inadequate…a store which is in an environment that is lower than I like to have for our customers." Russ Fowler, speaking of the regrettable decision to close, held out hope for a new store downtown, saying that "Battle Creek is a good town for us." After 1982, most customers were just as happy to take the twenty-seven-mile drive to Kalamazoo, where that city's Jacobson's had been expanded, remodeled and provided with additional parking.

Jacobson's 1970 East Lansing store was designed by veteran architecture firm Arthur O.A. Schmidt. The sumptuous interior was typical of Jacobson's, where sales were conducted over fine furniture, not a particle board counter. *Courtesy of the Ella Sharp Museum, Jackson, Michigan.*

A Capital Idea

*It is with great pride and the highest standards of good taste
that our new store will be presented.*
—*Jacobson's press release, November 1970*

Firmly established at the helm of his organization, Nathan Rosenfeld began the task of expanding Jacobson's into the department store he had always wanted to own. His plan was to expand not only horizontally, adding new lines, but also vertically, by entering more markets with new or acquired stores. In 1941, he asked Marjorie to accompany him on a brief trip north to East Lansing, a suburb of Michigan's capital city and home of Michigan State University. The purpose of the trip was to see a small women's clothing shop that had been offered for sale. In her memoirs, Marjorie states that, after inspecting the store, she asked her husband if it wouldn't be better for Jacobson's to start anew rather than taking over an existing business in the city. Rosenfeld apparently agreed with her position, for he soon negotiated a lease at 115 East Grand River Avenue, where the first new Jacobson's since the change of ownership was opened in 1941.

The store's exceptional customer acceptance and consistent sales growth are mirrored in the history of the expansions and renovations that characterized it. The store grew into adjacent space in 1944 and again annually from 1946 through 1948. In 1955, a bowling alley, which occupied the basement of the multi-tenant building, was acquired and became home to expanded offices and the children's shop. Two years later, an adjacent men's store was connected to the main store and became Jacobson's men's shop. This, too, proved inadequate by 1959, and the men's shop moved around the corner to Abbot Road, allowing space in the main building to be used to enlarge existing departments.

Rosenfeld's dream of a fine, full-line specialty store could never really be accommodated in the cobbled spaces of the store, as it grew along East Grand River, across from the MSU campus. Long before any new building project became a reality, he shrewdly began acquiring property one block east, for a future store that would live up to his ideal. In 1960, the East Lansing store suffered a setback when a part of its ceiling collapsed, damaging merchandise and exposing the poor conditions in the building at the time. A further setback to business was a flood, caused by a broken water main, which damaged the lower-level offices. In typically good-humored fashion, the office employees in the basement went about their jobs in galoshes until the damage was undone.

While the store was repaired and brought back into operation, an elaborate new Jacobson's was planned farther down East Grand River at the corner of Charles Street. After sixteen months of construction, the extravagant new Jacobson's opened on November 11, 1970. The press announcement for the new store stated that Jacobson's was presenting it "with great pride and the highest standards of good taste." With three levels above ground, and a basement below, the 117,000-square-foot store must have seemed like a pinnacle in Jacobson's development, and it surely bore out the press release's hyperbole.

The store's brick exterior, with accents of copper, set a traditional tone, while contemporary touches struck a fashionable and exclusive note. The interior featured, for the first time in East Lansing, full lines of Jacobson merchandise displayed around a dramatic, curved escalator well lined in brick and dotted with hanging plants. The attention to detail wasn't obvious only in the store's luxurious Designer Salon but also, not surprisingly, in the platform display just inside the front door. The eye-catching display was prepared featuring mannequins walking a pair of full-sized artificial Russian wolfhounds. Seeing the dogs on a pre-opening inspection, Nathan Rosenfeld wondered aloud why they didn't have license tags. The store's employees, ever attentive to detail—and to Rosenfeld's whims as well—saw to it that they were acquired and hung around the ever-so-chic dogs' necks in time for the grand opening the next day.

Customers were able to avail themselves of adjacent parking in a large deck located behind the store, which had opened the previous summer. A

A Capital Idea

The late Jaga Kell poses under a large crystal chandelier, at home in the glittering world of fashion and society. *Courtesy of the Ella Sharp Museum, Jackson, Michigan.*

two-level bridge connected the new garage to the store's upper two floors, the topmost of which housed a restaurant called the East Room, so-called not just because of its pseudo-Asian décor but also because it was on the east side of the building on East Grand River Avenue. The room was as popular for its excellent food as it was for its lavish atmosphere and panoramic treetop view of the Michigan State University campus across the street.

One employee's story stands out from this most elegant of stores. Jaga Kell, a prewar Polish socialite who grew up in Paris, served for many years as manager of the East Lansing Designer Salon. A blue-eyed blonde with Zsa Zsa Gabor looks, she came to the United States after World War II with her husband, Colonel Charles F. Kell, who had retired from the military

67

and was employed by Michigan State University. She spent her youth in the glittering world of European society and fashion but narrowly escaped internment and possible death in a concentration camp (a fate suffered by her first husband) by escaping to Germany as the war was coming to an end in Europe. She was forced to leave her son, ill with scarlet fever, in a hospital in Soviet-occupied Warsaw but under American medical supervision. For four months, she served as an interpreter for the American army, frantically trying to arrange a reunification with her son. An American officer who was returning to Poland for his Polish wife promised her that he would try to get

Architect's rendering of the rear (top) and front (bottom) of the older store on East Grand River Avenue, modernized and reconfigured to serve as Jacobson's new Store for the Home. *Courtesy of the Ella Sharp Museum, Jackson, Michigan.*

An integral part of the East Lansing store was the large parking deck behind the store. A two-level bridge allowed access to Jacobson's second and third floors. *Courtesy of the Ella Sharp Museum, Jackson, Michigan.*

her son back, which he did, dodging enemy fire on bicycle and foot until he could return the boy to Jaga. Sadly, he found that his own wife had been arrested and sent to Siberia.

Ever grateful for the generosity of this officer, Mrs. Kell stated in a *Lansing State Journal* interview, at the time of the store's opening, that "you never forget something like that, there is no way to ever repay." After spending time in postwar Europe, active in the Red Cross, she took up a fashion career with Jacobson's in East Lansing, reverting to the role of sophisticated socialite she had known so well in Paris and Warsaw, before the hostilities changed her life forever.

Once in its lavish new home, Jacobson's went about thoroughly renovating its old quarters for a new Store for the Home, which opened several months after the new building. The store was completely gutted inside and reconfigured to show Jacobson's newly acquired home

Asian-influenced decor of the East Room restaurant, which not only served as the East Lansing store's tearoom but also stayed open as a full-service eatery and event venue after retail business hours. *Courtesy of the Ella Sharp Museum, Jackson, Michigan.*

furnishings to the best effect. Both floors of the once deemed inadequate building provided twenty-three thousand square feet of space for the latest in furniture, carpeting and window treatments, as well as a Collector's Gallery of unusual decorative items.

Nathan Rosenfeld's dream of a regional chain of full-line specialty stores, second to none, operating in tandem with his strongly held principles of honesty, quality and service, would seem to have reached its ultimate form in the handsome buildings anchoring East Grand River Avenue in Lansing. Yet it would become obvious that dreams as wide and dynamic as his could never be represented by just one location.

The 1954 remodeling transformed the dowdy old Watson building into a sleek, modern emporium, with a chic, mid-century modern interior. Note the billboard advertisement for Grand Rapids competitor Wurzburg's. *Courtesy of the Ella Sharp Museum, Jackson, Michigan.*

Isn't That Just Grand?

This new store is a dramatic symbol of your continued acceptance of Jacobson's in Grand Rapids…of your faith in our ability to bring you unquestioned quality, service, and merchandise-rightness.
—*Jacobson's ad, Grand Rapids Press, November 11, 1954*

In 1943, while World War II raged on, the U.S. Army announced that it was closing the Military Weather School it had operated in Grand Rapids, which occupied, among other locations, space in Grand Rapids' *grande dame* hotel, the Pantlind. A local acquaintance of Nathan Rosenfeld's suggested that the two floors would make a great location for Jacobson's, situated, as they were, at the foot of Monroe Avenue, the city's main shopping thoroughfare, and connected to the lobby of Grand Rapids' best and most popular hotel.

In spite of the privations of wartime, the vacated space was redecorated for Jacobson's, and the store threw open its doors to the delight of shoppers in Michigan's furniture capital. Lively competition on Monroe Avenue ensued between Jacobson's and Herpolsheimer's, a part of Allied Stores, and locally owned department stores Steketee's and Wurzburg's.

Interior photos of this early store show that much of the hotel's classic architecture was retained and that the accommodation of a high-end fashion retailer was, in this case, more of a decorating job than a true remodeling of the space. Fabric, hung in a serpentine manner, was to

Grand Rapids, Jacobson's first occupied the north wing of the Pantlind Hotel's first two floors. A local architecture firm prepared this sketch showing new show windows and signage for the store. *Courtesy of the Ella Sharp Museum, Jackson, Michigan.*

Employees pose on the second floor of Jacobson's new Grand Rapids store in the Pantlind Hotel. The transitory nature of the space can be clearly seen. *Courtesy of the Ella Sharp Museum, Jackson, Michigan.*

substitute for walls to hide stockrooms from view. The plan took into account the difficulties of building during an international emergency, but it was not a makeshift one; the fabrics were to be of the best quality and coordinated with wall coverings and upholsteries selected for the store. However, three days before opening, it was revealed that the desired fabric would not be available in time. In a "master stroke" (pun intended), the display manager of the store contacted a local art school and asked if the students could paint the yardage on short notice. The finished job garnered welcomed press for Jacobson's and brought much appreciation for the students who carried out the work.

By 1949, when normalcy had returned and materials became plentiful, the store was again remodeled. The Pantlind Hotel, however, wanted to regain various leased spaces for its own operations, and Jacobson's went looking for a new location. It found new space in the existing Watson Building, on the other end of Monroe Avenue, near the dazzling new Herpolsheimer's store, which opened in 1949. The new Jacobson's, at thirty-six thousand square feet in size, was larger than its predecessor and offered an expanded range of merchandise, consistent with the company's growth at the time. News reports of the store's opening on August 11, 1954, made mention of the "brilliant interior decoration of woods, modern pastels, and other materials."

One aspect of the new Grand Rapids store offers insight into how Nathan Rosenfeld, and thus Jacobson's, handled everyday business relationships. One tenant of the Watson Building in 1954 was a furniture retailer whose lease did not expire until after Jacobson's was scheduled to open for business. Rosenfeld had construction works phased around the existing store and handled his competitor's move to a lease space across the street. The furniture store's manager at the time later became chairman of a local bank. He remained, for many years, grateful for the store's conduct in their earlier relations, and Jacobson's long remained a valued customer of his bank.

In the fall of 1965, an announcement was made that Jacobson's would augment its downtown operation with a new store in East Grand Rapids, in an area known as Gaslight Village, site of a former amusement park on Reed's Lake in the affluent and growing suburb. The downtown store, while immensely popular, had simply outgrown its location. Despite the fact that a men's store had been added and a customer parking lot had opened on an adjacent property, the store did not have the potential to keep up with Jacobson's growth at the time.

ready for you!

East Grand Rapids' new and
breathtakingly beautiful Jacobson's
...the enchanting new world of
fashion that has been designed
for you and your family, the
fashion-discerning shopper
of suburban Grand Rapids.

Jacobson's promoted the new East Grand Rapids store, and its signature colonnades, in the local press. *Courtesy of the Ella Sharp Museum, Jackson, Michigan.*

The new store opened in November 1966, with an image slightly different from its predecessors. A multilevel facility straddling a slope (which was used to provide access to the varying sales levels), it was enclosed by a brick colonnade topped by precast concrete arches. At 70,000 square feet, it was almost double the size of the downtown store and featured expanded selections. The interiors were among the first to show the change in decor toward the traditional, homelike atmosphere that came to be associated with Jacobson's in the late 1960s and 1970s. This eleventh pearl in the Jacobson chain proved popular enough that it was expanded again in 1974, to 105,000 square feet.

Mrs. Doris McPherrin was a Jacobson's employee who began in the early 1950s at the Pantlind Hotel and continued on to finish her career in East Grand Rapids. In 1980, she commented to the *Grand Rapids Press* that "it was the greatest feeling in the world to open the doors to the hotel, and step onto the thick, plush carpeting approaching Jacobson's entrance. With our continuous changes...one thing remains the same—Jacobson's still stands for quality and service. The only thing that changes is that we just keep getting older!"

With Jacobson's operating two stores in Grand Rapids, it is perhaps appropriate to detour north to mention one of the few early failures experienced by the retailer. After World War II, Nathan Rosenfeld decided

Isn't That Just Grand?

The East Grand Rapids store's design, and the slope of the five-and-a-half-acre site, allowed parking to feed into its various levels. Its elaborate custom store fixturing echoed the design of the colonnades on the exterior and gave the store a richly traditional atmosphere. *Courtesy of the Ella Sharp Museum, Jackson, Michigan.*

to locate a branch store in the resort town of Petoskey, Michigan, 185 miles north of Grand Rapids on the shores of Lake Michigan's Little Traverse Bay. Now popular year round due to the presence of ski resorts in the area, at the time it was strictly a summer destination, especially with tourists from across Lake Michigan.

Rosenfeld, however, did not want to follow the tradition of local retailers, who packed up and moved south in the winter. To operate a seasonal store would make staffing difficult, and he wanted full-time, dedicated employees for Jacobson's. The store opened for business in 1946 but soon after became problematic for the retailer. The trip north, to visit the stores or deliver merchandise, was difficult, especially in the winter. Stocking the branch became a nightmare, especially due to the fact that Jacobson's vaunted central distribution system had not yet been put into place.

In her memoirs, Marjorie Rosenfeld mentions their harrowing winter treks to the store, stating that "we could have used a dog sled." However, another factor may have influenced the unspectacular results that the store produced, though it cannot be substantiated. Rumors abound among Jake's former employees that the couple to whom Rosenfeld entrusted the operation of the store nurtured more than just customers,

The 1974 expansion added 50 percent more space to the East Grand Rapids store but continued the colonnade theme. Note the heavy wood doors in this sketch. *Courtesy of the Ella Sharp Museum, Jackson, Michigan.*

Isn't That Just Grand?

Rare photo of the almost completely forgotten Petoskey Jacobson's store, once located at 409 East Lake Street in the resort's downtown core. *Courtesy of the Ella Sharp Museum, Jackson, Michigan.*

but the bottle as well. How an astute businessman such as Rosenfeld could have misjudged the character of key employees goes against the truth of the tale, but the fact remains that he threw in the towel and shut down the store in 1949.

With a small but unfortunate detour behind it, though, Jacobson's had one more stop to make before entering Michigan's largest metropolitan market and confronting the retail behemoth that dominated it.

Nathan Rosenfeld's Saginaw "Superblock" project became a magnet for shoppers from northern Michigan. Among other expanded features, the "superblock" featured a completely new Store for the Home. *Courtesy of the Ella Sharp Museum, Jackson, Michigan.*

Saginaw, Superstore

If we were to prepare a balance sheet of Saginaw's Central Business District, it would have more assets than all of the new shopping centers combined.
—Nathan Rosenfeld, November 1976

Jacobson's entered the Saginaw market in 1926 with a short-lived lease department at Heavenrich Bros. & Co., an apparel store located on the corner of East Genesee Avenue and Germania (now Federal) Avenue. The operation was closed shortly after Moses Jacobson's death in 1929.

In 1943, Nathan Rosenfeld opened a small, five-thousand-square-foot store in the Michigan Bell Telephone building at 125–27 South Jefferson. Saginaw, the largest component of Michigan's "tri-city," which also includes Bay City and Midland, was not just a large retail market in its own right but also a gateway to Michigan's northland and a stopping-off point for travelers to the wealthy summer enclaves of Harbor Springs and Petoskey. That the decision to reopen in the tri-city area (also home of Dow Chemical Company, among other prosperous businesses) was a good one is demonstrated by the fact that the little shop was replaced with a fifty-three-thousand-square-foot store in 1955 at 400 Federal Street, across the street from its former home. Expanded again in 1959, the store became a major anchor in Saginaw's downtown business district.

Jacobson's grew in popularity, serving as it did a wide market area, and as in many locations, it bucked the trend of moving from the central business district and ultimately became a "destination" in itself, even while downtown

From 1955, Jacobson's occupied a typical, Mid-Century Modern store on Federal Street that was expanded by twelve thousand feet in 1959. *Courtesy of the Ella Sharp Museum, Jackson, Michigan.*

Saginaw declined. Out of this situation, Rosenfeld developed a plan for his Saginaw store that would make it the largest in the organization. In fact, the Saginaw "adventure," more than anything else that the store did, illustrated the commitment that Rosenfeld had to enhancing Michigan's central business districts.

Working with the City of Saginaw and the federal government, Rosenfeld assembled a team to propose a massive "superblock" in 1971. Centered on a vastly expanded 207,000-square-foot Jacobson's store, it filled the block bounded by Federal and Janes Avenues and South Baum and South Jefferson Streets. The city's Parking Deck No. 1, on Baum Street, was expanded from three to five levels and spanned across the street directly over the Jacobson store. When it proved impossible for the city to sell the bonds required to finance the project, Rosenfeld bought them and resold them at a discount to a Wall Street banking house. He sincerely believed that the $10,000 expense to do so was in the best interest of the city, of which Jacobson's was a part. Both colleagues and Saginaw press noted at the time that Rosenfeld accomplished a seemingly impossible task without grousing about the lack of participation by others in town or why the burden should fall on him to provide a public amenity. It was a case of, as he said at the time, "what was good for Saginaw was good for Jacobson's."

When Rosenfeld proposed the massive Saginaw project, the city was enjoying a downtown renewal that included a new civic center with arena and theater, a new federal building and expanded corporate facilities for some of the city's largest employers like Michigan Bell Telephone and Michigan National Bank. A new Downtown Saginaw Mall opened in 1973, with a completely new branch of local Saginaw retailer Morley Brothers as anchor.

Jacobson's was expanded gradually until the whole block was completed in November 1976. The large store included a Machus Sly Fox restaurant leased to the noted Detroit-area restaurateur and a more casual "Le Buffet" operated by Jacobson's. Expanded merchandise presentations included a large gourmet shop, with a license to sell wine, an electronics shop and a luggage department transformed into a comprehensive travel boutique. Likewise, fashion and home furnishings offerings were augmented and expanded in the elaborate new complex.

Speaking at the superblock's dedication, Rosenfeld reiterated his belief that downtown Saginaw had the potential to be "the" shopping center for not just its local communities but also the whole of the Lower Peninsula's northland, an area stretching up to the Straits of Mackinac. The *Saginaw News*, calling him a "zestful, highly respected merchandiser,"

The interior of the early Saginaw Jacobson's was likewise modern in character and occupied staggered levels that flowed into one another. *Courtesy of the Ella Sharp Museum, Jackson, Michigan.*

quoted Rosenfeld as saying, "If we were to prepare a balance sheet of Saginaw's central business district, it has more assets than all of the new shopping centers combined," and "we are going to do everything we can to participate in other developments between our store and the Civic Center." Specifically, ideas for a hotel and renovation of an adjacent apartment block into a shopping mall were put forth.

In the course of the Saginaw store's development, Rosenfeld noticed that the tri-city's newspapers, which were all owned by the Booth organization, forbade, for reasons he found ridiculous, cross-town advertising. A store like Jacobson's in Saginaw could not advertise in the *Bay City Times* and vice versa. Discovering that successive presidents of the publisher consistently upheld the policy, Rosenfeld, never one to mince words when commenting on something he considered foolish and inane, stated that "they can't get away with it" and had his staff search for a loophole in the policy. The papers did, they concluded, allow funeral monument fabricators to advertise

Jacobson's leased a large dining room and bar area to the Machus Sly Fox restaurant and operated its own eatery called Le Buffet in the large Saginaw store. *Courtesy of the Ella Sharp Museum, Jackson, Michigan.*

across city borders. Rosenfeld had advertising executive William T. Melms design an ad for a new "Remembrance Shop" at Jacobson's, featuring a headstone. He approached the publisher with the ad and, characteristically, won his argument to be able to advertise in Bay City.

Interestingly, Jacobson's prospered in the area and did become the destination store envisioned by Nathan Rosenfeld. The city's attempts at renewal, though, sadly fell flat. The downtown mall was a failure, and Morley's pulled out not long after Jacobson's opened. Business after business abandoned the troubled city center, and in later years, the Jacobson store was the only bright spot in a blighted downtown. Former employees and customers concur that the store's success, despite the adversities of its location, was due to a dedicated staff, who, by the sheer force of their efforts, had the ability to draw customers to the store, and in doing so, knew very well how to serve them with the courtesy and devotion that were a Jacobson's hallmark.

It is amusing to note that the Saginaw store did a uniquely brisk business in its lingerie department. Former employees recall that a brothel was well established in the neighborhood, and the ladies employed at it were very good customers for the store.

With established locations in many of Michigan's most important cities, Jacobson's looked east toward Detroit, where it first took a small step to establish itself in an immense market. For Jacobson's, though, it will be seen that little steps typically lead to very big things.

Jacobson's original, fifty-eight-foot-wide storefront in Grosse Pointe's "Village" shopping district. When it arrived, the street was a convenience center for the neighborhood, but that would soon change, as it developed into an exclusive shopping district. The interior of the original Jacobson's store provides insight into the nature of high-fashion apparel retailing in the 1940s. *Courtesy of the Ella Sharp Museum, Jackson, Michigan.*

Get to the Pointe

Here is a new store, a new type of store, born in the midst of the rapidly
changing world of today...but born with great promise for the future.
—Jacobson's ad in the Grosse Pointe News, November 1944

To say that the J.L. Hudson Company dominated the Detroit market
in the 1940s is a historically indisputable fact. Operating out of an
immense, twenty-one-story downtown flagship—a familiar pile of red bricks
dominating the Motor City's skyline—Hudson's featured every imaginable
merchandise line and customer service, including many restaurants and
specialties such as a contract furniture department dealing in office design
and hotel furnishings. Other retailers in town either gave up (the Ernst
Kern Co., a large competitor, went out of business in 1959) or eked out
an existence as a secondary player in the market, as did Hudson's major
downtown competitor, Crowley, Milner & Company. Hudson's was a very
fashion-oriented retailer, and it virtually owned the high-end apparel market
in the Detroit area, if not all of southeast Michigan.

In 1947, Hudson's upped the ante in this important classification by
gutting its seventh floor and creating the Woodward Shops, a store within
a store for exclusive designer fashion. To the degree that this innovation
was influenced by the appearance, in late 1944, of a Jacobson's store on
Kercheval Avenue in wealthy Grosse Pointe is difficult to ascertain. It is clear,
though, that Nathan Rosenfeld, Jacobson's owner, had an eye on the huge
Detroit market and decided that his neighborhood-style stores belonged near

Julius "Mr. Pete" D'Hondt was Jacobson's first employee in Grosse Pointe. His family maintained a relationship with Jacobson's for years, even selling their home to the store to facilitate expansion. *Courtesy of the Ella Sharp Museum, Jackson, Michigan.*

the well-heeled customers he identified for Jacobson's and not on Woodward Avenue in downtown Detroit, where Hudson's held court.

In November 1944, Jacobson's occupied a vacant space in the Tudor-style Tuttle & Clark building at 17036 Kercheval in the "Village" shopping area. From that point on, Jacobson's became an integral part of the tony suburb as to the manner born, and its residents responded to it enthusiastically. Jacobson's expanded again and again; within a year of its opening, the store had doubled in size by extending to St. Clair Avenue, and further additions aggrandized the store incrementally throughout the 1950s and early 1960s.

In 1952, a Home Decorative Shop opened a block away on the other side of Kercheval and was also enlarged several times. A fabric shop opened directly across from the apparel store in 1969. By this time, the apparel store was a conglomeration of ten different buildings behind a modern façade and included the popular St. Clair Room restaurant in its basement. Nathan Rosenfeld's desire to provide parking for customers was fulfilled by surface lots behind the two major buildings.

In 1973, plans were announced to enlarge and renovate the apparel store behind a unified, Colonial Williamsburg–style front. The city of Grosse Pointe, very much an exclusive residential enclave, did not respond enthusiastically at first to Jacobson's desire to build a parking deck behind the store on lots previously zoned for single-family houses. Rosenfeld responded by working with architect Arthur O.A. Schmidt in proposing a "Carriage House," with façades incorporating hints of the carriage house of the Governor's Palace in the historic Virginia town that had inspired the new store building's façades. After garnering approval for his plans, Rosenfeld entered into a typical agreement with Grosse Pointe, whereby it contributed taxes to a special assessment district that financed the construction of the deck, and as elsewhere, Jacobson's guaranteed the validation of parking stubs for its customers.

A detailed description of the remodeled store by architect Arthur O.A. Schmidt cited details incorporated into the design inspired by Williamsburg, including the circular "bullet" windows and wrought-iron balconies patterned after those on the original building of William and Mary College. Both the selection of the brick color and masonry details

By 1949, Jacobson's included the original Tuttle and Clark Building and a two-story addition that extended to St. Clair Street. *Courtesy of the Ella Sharp Museum, Jackson, Michigan.*

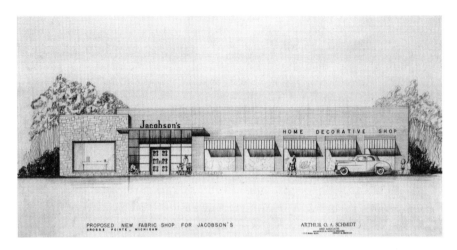

Jacobson's Home Decorative Shop opened across the street in 1952. The shop would later be expanded into a full-fledged Store for the Home, including home furnishings. *Courtesy of the Ella Sharp Museum, Jackson, Michigan.*

Dramatic night shot through the wooden doors of the Grosse Pointe Store for the Home. Solid wooden entry doors were a Jacobson's trademark. *Courtesy of the Ella Sharp Museum, Jackson, Michigan.*

A 1960s view of a very modern-looking Grosse Pointe Jacobson's. A portion of the roof of the original Tuttle & Clark building is visible above the parapet on the right. *Courtesy of the Ella Sharp Museum, Jackson, Michigan.*

such as soldier courses and dentils were inspired by historical structures as well. While the store complied with Grosse Pointe's desire for a historical vernacular, it had, by its very newness and large scale, a contemporary aspect as well.

In May 1974, an ad in the *Grosse Pointe News* hinted at Jacobson's pride in the splendid new store:

A wondrous thing has happened at Jacobson's. We're Williamsburg Colonial in Grosse Pointe...and lovelier than ever before...larger, lighter, brighter and with more space for greater selections of apparel for your entire family. Every innovation and expansion of departments, has been planned for your convenience and enjoyment...from shop-to-shop freedom of movement to authentic Colonial period interior design, from the new St. Clair Room restaurant with French doors opening onto formal gardens to the new D'Hondt pedestrian walkway. Ride the fascinating glass-enclosed elevator, the first of its kind in Michigan, to the second floor of fashions that include the Designer Salon and millinery. Or, take it to the lower level where the Miss J shop vibrates with color and the young mood. See the new departments debuting on the first floor: a stationery shop featuring personalized papers and informals, a fine jewelry selection, an expanded

The 1974 reconstruction mirrored the character of Grosse Pointe. Behind all the bricks and colonial detailing were ten separate buildings, added since 1944, but a view of the main accessories room in the new Grosse Pointe store, captures the homelike, but very chic, atmosphere that became typical of Jacobson's. *Courtesy of the Ella Sharp Museum, Jackson, Michigan.*

shoe salon. See the handsome Men's Shop, doubled in size to accommodate the Mr. J Shop and Prep Boys' clothing, its entrance flanked by porcelain lions. We're proud of our new appearance and want to share it with you. Come visit with us soon.

In fact, the Grosse Pointe store had long been recognized for the quality of the landscaping that embellished its grounds. The upkeep of this property was the work of Mrs. Irma D'Hondt, spouse of custodian and groundskeeper Julius "Pete" D'Hondt, who was the first employee Jacobson's hired in Grosse Pointe. Mrs. D'Hondt, born in Belgium in 1901 and affectionately known as "Mrs. Pete" by Jacobson's staff, lovingly embellished the exterior of the store with gardens. She was entirely responsible for the store winning the Grosse Pointe and Eastern Michigan Horticultural Society's competition for her work at Jacobson's, on four separate occasions.

Nathan Rosenfeld personally congratulates Irma D'Hondt at the dedication of D'Hondt Way, the public amenity behind the store named in her honor. *Courtesy of the Ella Sharp Museum, Jackson, Michigan.*

After her husband died, she became devoted to her work at Jacobson's and endeared the management not just by her gardening skills but also by her dedication to the store's appearance and upkeep. Her daughter, Bernice Grant, who also worked for Jacobson's for over forty years, recalls her mother's annual trips into manager Clarence Wascher's office, saying, in her Belgian accent, "Mr. Wascher, it is time to buy the Geraniums!" Her renowned green thumb no doubt stemmed in part from her ethnic heritage; in fact, her husband's family, who emigrated to the United States long before he met his wife while visiting relatives in Belgium, owned farmland in Grosse Pointe Woods that eventually became a part of the Lochmoor Country Club.

As a result, when the new store was finished in May 1974, the public passage between it and the "Carriage House," handsomely paved and ornamented with formal gardens, was named D'Hondt Way in her honor. At the dedication ceremony, when being congratulated by Nathan Rosenfeld, the seventy-three-year-old Mrs. D'Hondt reputedly asked him to "please don't make me stop working." She retired, reluctantly, in March 1982 and passed shortly afterward. D'Hondt Way was often the scene of al fresco fashion shows put on by Jacobson's and outdoor concerts by the Grosse Pointe Symphony Orchestra.

Lois Trost, who worked in Grosse Pointe from 1970, vividly remembers "Mrs. Pete," whom she says "was really something else. She took her job

Architect's rendering showing the Notre Dame Avenue side of the main store and the Williamsburg-inspired "Carriage House" at the rear. *Courtesy of the Ella Sharp Museum, Jackson, Michigan.*

Jacobson's traditional St. Clair Room was a popular place to eat in the Village. In good weather, the French doors opened to the gardens of D'Hondt Way. *Courtesy of the Ella Sharp Museum, Jackson, Michigan.*

seriously, and believe me, she didn't mess around. You wouldn't believe it, she'd climb a twelve-foot ladder just to get a cobweb, and in her seventies, yet!"

Among other memories of the store, which she describes as "marvelous," Mrs. Trost has special praise for Clarence Wascher, the store manager during the time she worked there. "He was so special; a wonderful man to work for. As an incentive, he'd organize 'mystery trips' for us. After work, a bus would pick us up and take us out to dinner to a special restaurant or to a lovely party arranged especially for us. Once we went all the way to Greenfield Village in Dearborn. I don't think there will ever be anything like it again."

All of the nuances of the Grosse Pointe store contributed to its remarkable public approval, and it became a true neighborhood store, identified in an almost possessive way by scores of Grosse Pointers, just as Nathan Rosenfeld had intended. This intimate atmosphere, combining not just the store's natural exclusivity but also its homelike traditional interiors and cordial service, developed in spite of its being a major player in a large retail market.

It would be six years after its opening in 1944 that Jacobson's would solidify its position by opening another store in a very different, but equally prosperous, corner of the Detroit metropolitan area.

By the 1970s, the Birmingham store consisted of (top to bottom) the main store, Children's Shops, Store for the Home and Men's Store. *Courtesy of the Ella Sharp Museum, Jackson, Michigan.*

Flagship Enterprise

You hear retailers say the reason they are leaving is that nobody is coming anymore because of the blight—and they were the ones who allowed the blight to happen in the first place. Our policy is to constantly improve our stores.
—Nathan Rosenfeld

On the day before the new Jacobson's store in Birmingham opened, a well-dressed woman tiptoed around the construction debris and packing material of the unfinished store to find the manager. She showed him the package she carried and a sales slip and asked for credit on a pair of shoes she had purchased two years earlier in Grand Rapids. They just didn't fit. "I've been waiting for two years for a Jacobson's store to open here," she said, "so I could take advantage of your legendary customer service." Wilber Mason, the bewildered manager, turned to Nathan Rosenfeld, who told him to fulfill the customer's request, offering his opinion that the store should never have sold ill-fitting merchandise to a customer. Many stores frame the first dollar made on opening day as a sign of good luck. In Birmingham, Rosenfeld had the credit slip framed as a sign of customers' confidence in Jacobson's.

It must have been a good omen, indeed, for the Birmingham store enjoyed a future full of financial success and the resultant expansion and improvement brought on by it. While every Jacobson's store was theoretically an equal in the mind of store management, the Birmingham store was an unofficial flagship, serving as it did one of the wealthiest suburban areas in America and eventually gracing the center of Birmingham with three separate buildings. In fact, store policy allowed a salesperson helping a

Photo of the original Birmingham store after it opened in 1950. *Courtesy of Elaine Coyne.*

customer in one structure to accompany his or her patron to one of the other stores (and back) if the patron so requested it. The store became the chain's biggest volume producer and also had the largest sales of high-end designer merchandise.

The store's presence in Birmingham began fairly humbly, after a site at 336 West Maple Road, at Bates Street, housing a vacant filling station was rezoned. The new apparel store structure actually reinforced and extended the city's business district to the west and opened in November 1950. Contemporary accounts in the Birmingham Eccentric describe the store as being built "of contemporary modern design, with glazed brick, crab orchard stone, granite and also air-conditioned."

Store manager Wilber Mason complained to Nathan Rosenfeld that he was having difficulty finding a maintenance man to care for the new facility. Rosenfeld devised an advertisement that he thought would attract the right individual, which, incidentally, was published after the position was filled. The "Key Man" ad, however, got much positive pre-opening publicity for Jacobson's because, for all its tongue-in-cheek humor, it was a concise statement about the respect for its employees that the store not only professed but put into action as well.

It was in Birmingham where another legendary event occurred. Rosenfeld visited prior to the opening of a separate shop for children and came upon the manager frantically trying to ready the store for customers. When

We're looking for the Key Man to work in our new Birmingham Store

(NO PHI BETA KAPPA's)

Wanted immediately — man without college degree to assume position of greatest responsibility in the newest Jacobson store. Excellent opportunity to work with the most intricate of equipment; including thermostats, draft controls, humidifiers, and percipitrons. Must be good business opener—and closer. Chance to work-up . . . from basement to top level every day. Should be qualified as aggressive pusher for vital mop-up operations which otherwise would be assumed by store manager if key man is not procured. Anyone accepted will be able to wax important at all hours with the entire area within his sweep. His outlook should be clear and well defined—especially through plate glass. Here is the opportunity to practice meteorology by control of the sun with awnings, the humidity with General Electric, and snow with a shovel. College graduates may be considered as a last resort if well-mannered and with some indication of not-forgotten native intelligence. Apply Mr. Mason, who will revert to store manager if you are accepted.

Jacobson's

MAPLE AT BATES   BIRMINGHAM

This advertisement is being published as a matter of record only—since we were fortunate enough to have already filled the position.

"Key Man" ad in the Birmingham Eccentric, dating from Jacobson's opening in Birmingham, 1950. *Courtesy of the Ella Sharp Museum, Jackson, Michigan.*

he asked Rosenfeld for an additional employee to help mop floors and cart refuse, it was the president himself who went to work, explaining, "If I'm not good enough to do floors, I'm not good enough to run this company."

The store grew in stages. In October 1953, a new home decorative shop opened at 325 North Woodward Avenue. A spate of improvements in 1956 provided more space for the home decorative shop, a beauty salon and a separate children's shop at North Woodward and Willits Streets. In 1962, a men's store was added to the home store, which itself was duly enlarged. Then, in 1963, the apparel store got a new second floor, which extended over the rear parking lot, thus providing covered parking for customers.

With Jacobson's entry into the furniture market, a major addition was made to the Store for the Home in 1967. The Daly Brothers furniture store on Woodward Avenue in Bloomfield Hills was closed, and its merchandise was showcased in downtown Birmingham instead, coordinated with Jacobson's related lines of home furnishings merchandise.

Five years later, the apparel store received a complete makeover, giving it the warmly traditional image that many Jacobson's stores had acquired by that time. Birmingham mayor William Saunders welcomed the rich terra cotta brick and copper-clad structure, saying, "The expansion proposed by Jacobson's is just the kind of thing we were looking for...since it is an entrance way to the city." The expansion confirmed the flagship status of the store, bringing it to 183,000 square feet in floor area. Later improvements at the children's shop and the Store for the Home gave them exteriors similar to the apparel store, making Jacobson's Birmingham store into a complete ensemble of handsome retail facilities.

Models pose in the latest Jacobson's fashions around a sweeping staircase on the second floor of Jacobson's apparel store after its 1972 remodeling. *Courtesy of the Ella Sharp Museum, Jackson, Michigan.*

Flagship Enterprise

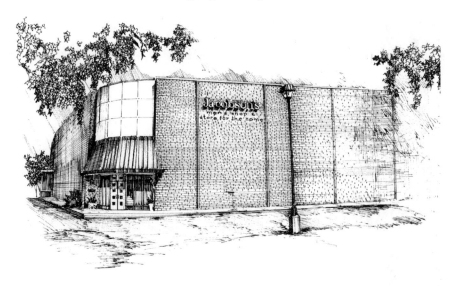

The rear entrance to Jacobson's Birmingham Store for the Home was caught in pen-and-ink by a store artist. *Courtesy of the Ella Sharp Museum, Jackson, Michigan.*

During the store's long history of expansion, Nathan Rosenfeld addressed the parking issue in the city as he had done elsewhere. Mark Rosenfeld, his son, who joined Jacobson's in 1972 and went on to become president and chief executive officer of the store, remembers that his father made over one hundred trips to Birmingham to negotiate parking proposals with the city. These meetings resulted in a comprehensive, well-financed and sustainable parking system that didn't benefit only Jacobson's, which validated parking tickets for its customers.

A major goal of the system in Birmingham, as elsewhere, was to make the parking inexpensive enough to allow the central business district to compete with the expanses of convenient parking available at outlying shopping centers. The elder Rosenfeld often remarked that "we have to have a strong downtown," and when questioned about the fact that his efforts were beneficial to his competitors, he responded that "the more competition, the better. If we can't stand the traffic, it's our fault. But if we don't have traffic, we're in trouble."

By making such a significant investment in downtown Birmingham, Jacobson's showed its faith in the Detroit market, which it began to circle with its chic and graceful stores. While it would not open another completely new store for ten more years after the Birmingham debut, Jacobson's wasn't done expanding in Michigan's outstate cities by a long shot.

Jacobson's Kalamazoo store was expanded from a simple modern building into a lavish composition of daringly detailed and richly toned brickwork that was only hinted at in architect's sketches. *Courtesy of the Ella Sharp Museum, Jackson, Michigan.*

I've Got a Store in Kalamazoo

We grow this way: we will never open a new store in any year where we would have to slow down the pace of constantly improving the stores we have.
—Nathan Rosenfeld

In the 1950s, Victor Gruen, the émigré Austrian architect, literally invented the shopping mall as we know it. His breakthrough work was Northland Center in suburban Detroit, but his creative mind, which was nurtured in the vicinity of the fabulous Ringstrasse of late nineteenth-century Vienna, wasn't only fixated on suburbia. For the betterment and well-being of central cities, he prescribed a program of pedestrianization of major shopping streets and the development of encircling access roads with associated parking. Detailed studies were produced by his office for Fort Worth, Fresno and, in 1958, Kalamazoo, with the professed aim of countering runaway suburbanization and bringing new life and longevity to city centers. Specifically, the "Kalamazoo 1980" plan proposed a Ringstrasse-like access road around downtown Kalamazoo, new perimeter parking and a lively pedestrian zone at the core of the city.

Consequently, the Kalamazoo city council adopted only the portion of the plan that they could afford with the help of downtown businesses, and the Kalamazoo Mall became reality when two blocks of Burdick Street were closed and landscaped in 1959. Looking back at lively and colorful postcards, appreciative newspaper articles and the experience of Gilmore Brothers, the large department store that anchored the northern end of the mall, the impact and success of the mall at the time is abundantly clear.

So it was for Jacobson's, which, after years of expanding and improving its existing retail locations, set its sights on the exciting developments in downtown Kalamazoo. Jacobson's commissioned a new store at 359 South Burdick, on the site of the disused Central Fire Station. The sleek, modern structure, similar in appearance to other Jacobson's buildings from the era, sat like a jewel at the southern limit of the mall, which was expanded southward to meet it. Intriguingly, the Jacobson's site had the advantage of being situated at the end of the mall and still had convenient automobile access along Lovell Street. A common criticism of pedestrian malls like Kalamazoo is that while they did improve the visual environment along a major street, they seriously hampered traffic patterns and access to the retailers, which depended on traffic in order to survive. These effects were pronounced in Kalamazoo due to the fact that only the street improvements were implemented, while the crucial parking and access routes were put on the back burner.

When the forty-three-thousand-square-foot branch opened in August 1960, Nathan Rosenfeld was certainly enthusiastic about its prospects due to the community's inherent wealth, but he remained concerned about the fact that only the pedestrian mall part of Gruen's plan was adopted. Plans for better vehicular access for the mall and the Austrian architect's parking recommendations remained unaccomplished. For over two decades, Rosenfeld would be an advocate for improved and increased access to ample parking at the Kalamazoo Mall's perimeter.

Nonetheless, the new store made a big impact on the Kalamazoo market, dominated for so long by Gilmore's, and Jacobson's readily became a major anchor of the Kalamazoo Mall. In time, the expansion and improvement characteristic of Jacobson's stores in the era took place in Kalamazoo as well. In 1966, Jacobson's opened a "Campus Shop" near the Western Michigan University campus, at 2702 West Michigan Avenue. Located in the Campus Theater Building, it housed both the store's men's shop and the young women's Miss J Shop.

Old articles in the *Kalamazoo Gazette* go far in revealing the Kalamazoo customer's appreciation for Jacobson's unique style in their home city. Patrons stated that they enjoyed "shopping for elegant clothing for day and evening wear" and "walking proudly out of the store with purchases packed neatly in a silver Jacobson's box." One customer related a story in the newspaper about the time her macramé purse snagged a brassiere, which she unwittingly carried throughout the store. The incident may have caused her daughter, with whom she was shopping, to laugh, but

I've Got a Store in Kalamazoo

An old W.T. Grant store made way for Kalamazoo's large (thirty-thousand-square-foot) Store for the Home, presaging the later brick exterior applied to the main store. *Courtesy of the Ella Sharp Museum, Jackson, Michigan.*

she also recalled fondly that the humor of the situation was shared by the ever-friendly Jacobson's saleswoman who restocked the runaway garment. Later, the store's Garden Place restaurant elicited nostalgic comments about "special occasions in that delightful eatery up there. The food was always attractively prepared and tasteful."

In 1969, Jacobson's announced that it had purchased the location of the former W.T. Grant store at 215 South Burdick on the Kalamazoo Mall and planned to open a thirty-thousand-square-foot Store for the Home. Grant's old but handsome limestone Art Deco façade came down and was replaced with a colonnade of brick arches that hinted at the new look of Jacobson's stores of the 1970s. When the Store for the Home opened in 1970, Jacobson's was able to present its full line of merchandise in Kalamazoo.

While the store prospered and even drew customers from Jacobson's nearby, but smaller, Battle Creek store, Rosenfeld had not been able to make an acceptable impact on the parking situation downtown. In 1979, however,

Nathan Rosenfeld reviews plans at the Kalamazoo construction site in 1978. *Courtesy of the Ella Sharp Museum, Jackson, Michigan.*

The new image of the Kalamazoo Jacobson's store, with its deeply corbelled brickwork and chamfered window recesses, was mildly reminiscent of the nature-inspired work of Catalan architect Antonio Gaudi. *Courtesy of the Ella Sharp Museum, Jackson, Michigan.*

the store acquired the former Schensul's Cafeteria Building next door and proposed a thirty-five-thousand-square-foot addition, connecting to a new civic parking deck at the rear, finally fulfilling the original Kalamazoo Mall's plan for perimeter parking. As in other cities, Jacobson's executed agreements making the structure a reality and was able to achieve Rosenfeld's desire to improve the parking situation in downtown Kalamazoo.

The new store opened gradually throughout late 1979 and early 1980. When the scaffolding came down, it revealed a new brick façade, in keeping with Jacobson's image, but the building's elaborate masonry work was strikingly different, with deep cornices, dramatically recessed windows and an unusual corner entrance on the mall. The work of local architects Diekema Hamann Associates, the structure was vaguely reminiscent of the work of Catalan architect Antonio Gaudi.

Keith Houck, Jacobson's director of store planning, described the work involved in an interview in the *Kalamazoo Gazette* and spoke about the reconstruction process, ending his comments with the statement that "we'll sure be happy when this whole project is finished." It was indeed completed and provided the Kalamazoo Mall with a handsome and popular exclamation point at its southern end. The store escaped serious damage in the terrible tornado that hit Kalamazoo on May 13, 1980. The force of the storm collapsed the rear façade of competitor Gilmore Brothers and resulted in the tragic loss of five lives.

Jacobson's had not opened a new store location in the ten years before it found a home in Kalamazoo. Before long, however, it would set its feet down again, to complete a necklace-like chain around the city of Detroit, Michigan's biggest metropolitan area.

The interior of Jacobson's Dearborn store featured large-scale design gestures such as the "bull in a china shop" visible in the store's gift gallery, and a full-size reproduction of a cannon in the Spanish Colonial men's shop. *Courtesy of the Ella Sharp Museum, Jackson, Michigan.*

Triple Crown

The biggest investment a retailer needs today is a magnificent plant.
—Nathan Rosenfeld

A description in the *Dearborn Press & Guide* in October 1964, under the headline "They Gaze in Awe," vividly described the new Dearborn Jacobson's, saying, "The entire store is much like an elegant mansion with each department an entity in itself—each with the air of a separate salon… with its own select decor of chests, bureaux, and tables displaying goods; couches and chairs are available to those with weary feet or for husbands to wait while their wives take their selections from a vast array of quality merchandise" and that "chandeliers replace standard department store lighting; French provincial couches take the place of chairs in the shoe salon; alcoves and curved displays replace the usual row on row of clothing racks." The article also glowingly reported that "stair cases rise spirally, circling around a fountain bubbling from the lower level to the top floor…the escalator joined the three levels encased in semi-circular brick walls topped with an opaque sky light."

This beautiful store, the third in the Detroit area, and a landmark in the West Dearborn shopping district, stretched a whole city block along Michigan Avenue. Once again the work of architect Arthur O.A. Schmidt, it was the first comprehensive Jacobson's store in a new building, and its elegant style of contemporary design with traditional details was a pacesetter for things to come. Colorful Dearborn mayor Orville Hubbard and city councilman

A portrait captured the Dearborn groundbreaking ceremony in July 1963. Nathan Rosenfeld is visible in the middle; Russ Fowler is to his left but partially hidden. Wielding shovels are councilman Irving F. ImOberstag and Mayor Orville Hubbard. *Courtesy of the Ella Sharp Museum, Jackson, Michigan.*

Irving F. ImOberstag worked closely with Nathan Rosenfeld to bring the store to Dearborn, on a derelict site containing an electrical substation and a deconsecrated Episcopal church. City officials were quick to point out that Jacobson's built the elaborate store in Dearborn, while Detroit's J.L. Hudson Company only saw fit to erect a freestanding budget store in their town. Jacobson's believed the store to be an "important community statement" that enhanced its own (and Nathan Rosenfeld's) vision of the organization as a group of neighborhood stores, not a mere chain.

Once again, an aspect of a Jacobson's store showed the droll side of its owner's character. Rosenfeld had a huge, life-size, wrought iron bull installed in the middle of the store's china shop, as a tongue-in-cheek reminder of a popular adage. "That was Nathan's baby," recalls Jim Zuleski. "He never ceased to get a kick out of his 'bull in a china shop' and made sure he pointed it out whenever visiting the store." Such large-scale decorative touches were common features of the branch, like the reproduction antique cannon and oversize blueprint drawing of it that signified the Cannon Shop for young men.

The fact that the store was all of a piece gave it a peerless character, even among Jacobson's stores. The brick-enclosed escalator well (see

Architect Arthur O.A. Schmidt produced a rendering showing the block-long store along Michigan Avenue. The carport was not executed as illustrated. *Courtesy of the Ella Sharp Museum, Jackson, Michigan.*

frontispiece), the Spanish Colonial–style men's shop and the delightful restaurant opening off a lounge at the Top of the Fountain were just a few of the features that contributed to its singular atmosphere. As part of the Jacobson's organization, the store, over its lifetime, garnered a reputation as a training ground; a list drawn up for Jacobson's 125th anniversary in 1993 named nineteen Dearborn employees who went on to gain managerial or supervisory positions in other branches or at the company's Jackson headquarters.

Interesting stories, as has already been seen, have been recorded about practically every one of Jacobson's stores; Dearborn is no exception. For example, a tale has circulated for years about a phone call informing the store that a fabulously wealthy Saudi prince was to visit Jacobson's with a forty-person entourage. Management, not wanting to disappoint a celebrity customer, took steps to make sure there were interpreters on hand, as well as a full staff to serve the group, but the call ultimately turned out to be a hoax.

At the time of the Dearborn opening, Daly Brothers Furniture had been an established fixture on west Michigan Avenue since 1917. Undoubtedly, it was Nathan Rosenfeld's habit of getting to know his retail neighbors that led, in 1967, to the purchase of the fifty-year-old furniture business by Jacobson's. At the time, a Jacobson's press release noted Daly Brothers' "quality image in the home furnishings field" and "strong customer acceptance of its fine furniture lines."

Before long, the store was remodeled and renamed Jacobson's Store for the Home, giving the company a niche in the furniture and floor-coverings markets. This business was then systematically integrated into

A close-up image illustrates the neoclassical detailing of the otherwise modern store. *Courtesy of the Ella Sharp Museum, Jackson, Michigan.*

Jacobson's became a full-line specialty department store when it acquired the fifty-year-old Daly Brothers Furniture Co., a few doors away from the Dearborn store. *Courtesy of the Ella Sharp Museum, Jackson, Michigan.*

Jacobson's operations in other cities as well. A second Daly location on Woodward Avenue in Bloomfield Hills was closed when an expanded Store for the Home replaced it as a part of an expansion of the Birmingham Jacobson's store.

By the late 1960s, Jacobson's had become a full-line specialty department store—and a tremendously well-liked and respected one at that. The boundless wealth of ideas that Nathan Rosenfeld had for his company just wouldn't let up, as will be seen, even when the sixty-six-year-old merchant took a vacation.

The Longwood store was the first newly-built Jacobson's in the Sunshine State. It carried on the Colonial home image of the Yankee Traveler, even though it at first took the Proctor Shop name. The typically elegant interior made rich use of homelike store furnishings manufactured in the Unites States and Canada. *Courtesy of the Ella Sharp Museum, Jackson, Michigan.*

Snowbird Store

Look at all of those Michigan license plates. I wonder how many of them have Jacobson's accounts? Shouldn't we give them somewhere to use them down here?
—*Marjorie Rosenfeld, quoting her husband, Nathan*

Like many residents of midwestern states, the Rosenfelds were enticed to winter in Florida, especially after the busy 1968 Christmas season. Visiting friends in Sarasota, on the way to a family vacation, they soon found their own apartment and became typical "snowbirds"—Michiganians spending winter months in the more hospitable Florida climate.

Unlike most of them, though, Nathan Rosenfeld soon tired of Gulf breezes and beachfront dining and took a long, critical look at the retail trade in Sarasota. In the 1930s, before purchasing Jacobson's, Rosenfeld had prepared a report for Allied Stores on Florida's retail market, in which he concluded that Florida would experience an unprecedented growth market for retailers in the future. Allied responded by purchasing Tampa's renowned Maas Brothers and creating an offshoot of Boston's Jordan Marsh Company in Miami to serve the Sunshine State's east coast.

On St. Armand's Circle, the very tony shopping district of the exclusive keys west of Sarasota proper, Rosenfeld took an extraordinary interest in a store called the Yankee Traveler, founded in 1957 by John and Bernadine Haman, which specialized in home furnishings but offered women's fashions as well. A Yankee Traveler ad stated that the light blue building on the Circle *looks like a home…and it is! It is home to many clients, customers, and visitors who delight in the backgrounds for living in our Design and Décor Shop, in the Patio Gift Shop, and in the three model apartments and Art Gallery on the second floor. It is home to those who come to see and shop in our Women's Fashion and Accessory Shop. There is always a light in the window of The Yankee Traveler to welcome you "home."*

Recognizing the Yankee Traveler's commitment to quality merchandise and customer service and that it served what he recognized as "the Jacobson's customer," he offered to buy the store, and Jacobson's Florida division was born. The press release explaining the Yankee Traveler deal extolled the virtues of the "distinctively unusual store" and called it a "logical acquisition." Prophetically, the announcement stated in no uncertain terms that "we plan to use this acquisition as the nucleus of a regional group of specialty stores in Florida.

With the Yankee Traveler in Jacobson's hands, Rosenfeld began to dream about more stores across the Sunshine State, the west coast of which was in reality an enclave of midwesterners who had either relocated for the tropical climate or simply visited during part of the year. Indeed, the plan was to call all further stores in Florida Yankee Traveler, but it was found that the name

You are invited to visit

the YANKEE TRAVELER
St. Armand's Circle — Sarasota, Florida

We are pleased to announce that The Yankee Traveler, a distinctively unusual home furnishings and fashion specialty store in Sarasota, Florida, is now a part of Jacobson's. The next time you travel south, we invite you to visit The Yankee Traveler and discover the same fine quality, customer service and hospitality that has become a Jacobson tradition in Michigan. Of course, your Jacobson charge account identification card will be honored at The Yankee Traveler.

Jacobson's

Advertisement announcing the acquisition of the Yankee Traveler to Michigan customers, who often wintered in Florida. *Courtesy of the Ella Sharp Museum, Jackson, Michigan.*

Snowbird Store

The Yankee Traveler looked like a large, Colonial-style home on St. Armand's Circle. In fact, it became a full-scale Jacobson's store with expansion to the side and rear. *Courtesy of the Ella Sharp Museum, Jackson, Michigan.*

wasn't a properly registered trademark, and there was also a trailer park in the state called Yankee Traveler. From the time of the purchase, the St. Armand's Circle store was known as Jacobson's Yankee Traveler and, later, simply as Jacobson's.

The original, home-like store facing St. Armand's Circle had a Decor and Design shop on the first floor, along with a Patio Gift Shop and various women's fashion salons. In addition to the art gallery on the second floor, one of the three furnished apartments was occupied as a residence by the owners but was also used to show furniture after they had gone down in the morning to greet their customers. Eventual remodeling and expansion of the store changed the merchandise from a concentration on furniture to a mix reflecting the more fashion-oriented Jacobson's practice, but since it grew mostly toward the back, the one-of-a-kind shop maintained its distinctive image on the Circle.

The many long-term employees of the store reveled in tales of the rich and eccentric who patronized it, from a woman who furnished a new home every year (and once used a china cabinet sideways when, after delivery, it was found to be too tall for her dining room ceiling), to another who "held court" every day in the store and bought over twenty robes at a time during a trunk show and heirloom, hand-beaded evening bags at a rate of one a month for several years. These employees enjoyed the same cordial, intimate relationship with Jacobson's and its customers as their northern

Jacobson's

Proctor
Shop

When you are in the Orlando area this winter, plan to visit us at Jacobson's Proctor Shop in Winter Park. You'll find the same quality apparel for women and children, and the same courteous service you enjoy at Jacobson's in Michigan. Of course, you can use your Jacobson charge account at the Proctor Shop.

in Winter Park, Florida

Jacobson's advertised the Proctor Shop to Michigan credit card holders, since many of them, too, were "snowbirds." *Courtesy of the Ella Sharp Museum, Jackson, Michigan.*

counterparts—mitigated by the climate, of course. Business dropped off annually in the summer, so the store was closed a half hour earlier, but employees were still paid for a forty-hour workweek. Rosenfeld believed it was fair enough compensation for hard work during the busy winter season.

The concept of a network of Florida stores took a step toward reality in 1972, when Nathan Rosenfeld "discovered" the wealthy Orlando suburb of Winter Park. Founded in 1882, the gracious enclave included five small lakes and a lush central park surrounding its railroad station. The retail center of the town clustered around Park Avenue. In 1948, Eve Proctor, a former buyer for Bonwit Teller in New York, founded a fashion shop in Winter Park and named it after herself. Working with her son, Richard, she was able to expand the store across the street to 339 Park Avenue and build a retail complex, the Proctor Center, which also housed a children's shop, a florist, a beauty salon and a gift shop. In 1972, Rosenfeld purchased the store and leased the rest of the building to house an expanded operation known as Jacobson's Proctor Shop.

The Proctor Center Building also housed the Florida regional offices of Jacobson's, but these were later moved to a completely new Jacobson's store in Longwood, a western suburb of Orlando. When the offices outgrew that location, a new Florida Office and Distribution Center was built in

The Proctor Shop eventually became simply Jacobson's. *Courtesy of the Ella Sharp Museum, Jackson, Michigan.*

1982 in Winter Park, modeled on its Jackson predecessor. By the time that Jacobson's had become established in Florida, stores like Saks Fifth Avenue and Bonwit Teller had long been a part of the retail scene on the state's east coast. Jacobson's differed by maintaining a separate staff of buyers in Florida and, as a result, was able to better serve the state than its New York–based competition, whose buyers simply sent down merchandise they thought Floridians would buy.

Sigrid Wolf worked as a staff supervisor for Estee Lauder Corp. before being asked by Jacobson's to become a cosmetics and fragrances buyer in Florida. Among other things, one of her fondest memories of working in the Florida regional offices was of visits by Russ Fowler. "Whenever he was at the Florida regional office, he'd pop in to say, 'Sigi, are you still buying all that stinky stuff?' and I'd say, 'Yes, Mr. Fowler, you know I am and you know how we both love it!'" In fact, it was a bit of a point of contention, since Jacobson's prided itself on being a fine apparel retailer, but cosmetics was traditionally a number one volume category for the store. In spite of the fact that Fowler's pre-Jacobson's retail background included experience in the cosmetics market, the volume of cosmetics sold versus fashion apparel was a sore point. Wolf also makes light of the differences between the employees of the Florida division and their counterparts up north, saying, "My boss, Ron Roberts, loved to joke about the differences between the North and South buying groups' images, which, of course, was reflected in our merchandise assortments, too. He said the northern buyers and management looked like 'insurance salespeople with their navy suits and Peter Pan collars,' and we looked 'all Florida flash and trash with our bright colors!' Interestingly, we were more profitable than the Michigan stores for the last years."

The Longwood store itself occupied a small shopping center called Longwood Village. The forty-five-thousand-square-foot branch was Jacobson's first purpose-built store in Florida and combined the Colonial style of the original Yankee Traveler with the brick-built traditions of Jacobson's Michigan stores. The store opened in January 1975. Sigrid Wolf

a bright new Jacobson's has dawned
our second Orlando area store is now
open for your shopping convenience
at Longwood Village, US 4 at 434. . .
it's a total fashion environment for
men, women and children and for your
home, in addition to a complete beauty
salon. You've been so nice to us all
these years in Winter Park, we thought
we'd do it again. Now we are "two".

Jacobson's
PROCTOR SHOPS

LONGWOOD
US 4 at 434

WINTER PARK
339 Park Avenue North

Jacobson's ad announcing the opening of the Longwood Village store in 1975. *Courtesy of the Ella Sharp Museum, Jackson, Michigan.*

The 1977 North Palm Beach store in Oakbrook Square took on an altogether more Mediterranean look befitting its location. It was eventually doubled in size by the addition of a second floor. *Courtesy of the Ella Sharp Museum, Jackson, Michigan.*

herself remembers "how beautiful Jacobson's stores and visuals were" with this example:

I was making a store visit with my Oscar de la Renta rep, who commented, "This is why I just adore your stores (in front of an accessories and women's wear display)…you always have such uniquely beautiful merchandise." We did always strive to that end, but the merchandise in that particular display, I knew, was also available at Burdine's since I had been doing some comparative shopping there a few days prior! We were exemplary in our presentations as well as service, and it truly did make a big difference to the customers.

With a store on Florida's Gulf Coast, and two in the Orlando area, Jacobson's turned to the Sunshine State's east coast for its next expansion, in spite of the fact that the area was not as popular with midwesterners who would be familiar with Jacobson's. Taking an anchor position in the new Oakbrook Fashion Square in North Palm Beach, Jacobson's opened in December 1977, and the press release associated with the event mentioned the store's "light, airy elegant Florida feeling with touches of regional textures" and the soft sculpture artwork in the children's shop showing the animal kingdom at play. In spite of the presence of the exclusive Worth Avenue shopping area in Palm Beach proper, with its branches of New York stores, the new Jacobson's was a runaway success.

In reality, its proximity to Palm Beach itself meant that the store was a favorite with celebrities. Marjorie Rosenfeld noted in her history chronicles that Liberace frequented the store, and on one occasion, a saleswoman, learning that her customer's late husband was a football coach, inquired as to which high school team he had led. "Why, I'm Mrs. Vince Lombardi!" was the woman's reply. The label of the designer shoe that the saleswoman had to extract from her mouth, however, has gone unrecorded.

The North Palm Beach store changed its appearance when it was doubled in size to ninety thousand square feet by the addition of a second floor in 1987.

In 1980, Jacobson's added two more stores on the Gulf Coast. The first, in Osprey, Florida, midway between Sarasota and Venice, opened on October 1, 1980, and occupied a thirty-one-thousand-square-foot space in the Southbay Fashion Center. The smaller Clearwater store, in Northwood Plaza, an open-air center around a European-style courtyard with a lighted pool and an arched bridge over cascading water, was a

The Clearwater and Osprey stores, opened in 1980, occupied small but exclusive shopping centers in affluent communities. *Courtesy of the Ella Sharp Museum, Jackson, Michigan.*

women's clothing and accessories branch but was later enlarged into a full-size Jacobson's store. Both of these Florida stores provided a new home for the long-term Jacobson's employees who moved from Michigan to take positions as their managers.

While not in downtowns like their northern counterparts, the new Florida branches weren't deprived of Nathan Rosenfeld's attention. In their planning, he was instrumental in selecting the locations and

The 1982 Florida regional office was located on Driggs Drive, not far from the Orlando Executive airport, from which buyers could depart on trips to the Florida stores. *Courtesy of the Ella Sharp Museum, Jackson, Michigan.*

encouraging fine restaurants to join as tenants in order to ensure amenities for his customers. The press release announcing the stores' openings quoted him as saying, "Jacobson's Clearwater and Southbay operations will combine all the distinctive features and personalized customer service of our stores," and they "offer expanded service to our customers who are accustomed to shopping at Jacobson's." Reading between the lines, it is clear that by this time Jacobson's was an established feature of the Florida retail scene.

In Florida, Marjorie Rosenfeld's contribution to the company cannot be discounted. For much of her professional life, she worked in Jacobson's import department deftly handling paperwork relating to cross-border purchases of the store. In 1957, she and Nathan took their family on an extensive European tour while signing contracts with commissionaires who formed a liaison between the store and the continent's leading fashion houses.

With the couple's acquisition of a pied à terre in Florida, Marjorie took an active role in the setup and operation of the Florida stores as well. Her memoirs describe one-off events like a Clearwater fashion show she arranged on a moment's notice, but one of her ongoing responsibilities was to set up the stores' receiving and stock rooms and conduct employee training for their proper utilization. No doubt she was able to carry out her husband's wishes with regard to these areas, since he was a stickler for

The Fort Myers store opened onto a courtyard in the Bell Tower shopping complex. Its design was altogether contemporary, albeit with a Spanish influence. *Courtesy of the Ella Sharp Museum, Jackson, Michigan.*

efficiency and organization in Jacobson's behind-the-scenes areas. Rosenfeld even coined a term, "convenienating," to describe his philosophy of stock room organization.

Jacobson's growth and expansion in Florida, plus its organizational structure and business practices, which sought to serve the market directly rather than from the company's Jackson headquarters, meant that the regional offices, which had moved to the Longwood Village shopping center in 1976, became inadequate by the early 1980s. Jacobson's built a new Florida regional office and distribution center on Driggs Drive in Winter Park. Opening in 1982, the facility was well located with regard to the burgeoning Jacobson's presence in the Sunshine State.

The offices were convenient to Orlando Executive Airport, which became important in later years when Don Hathaway, Jacobson's vice-president of Florida stores, convinced northern management that the lease of a six-seater airplane would improve efficiency and streamline travel between Jacobson's far-flung network of stores in the division.

The same year also saw a store open in Fort Myers, Florida, on the Gulf Coast. Also located in a small shopping center, this time called the Bell Tower, it was, at least on the exterior, a low-key contemporary design influenced by Florida's Mediterranean-inspired architecture.

Jacobson's expanded rapidly in Florida, opening a grandiose neoclassical store, in 1983. It was followed by the expansion of the small Clearwater unit into a full-scale store. *Courtesy of the Ella Sharp Museum, Jackson, Michigan.*

In 1983, a large, full-line Jacobson's store opened in Jacksonville, in the Grande Boulevard shopping center in the city's southern suburbs. At one time, the store, housed in an elaborate, neoclassical building with a semicircular porte-cochère, became the highest-grossing location in Jacobson's Florida operation.

Since the time of its inception, it was intended to expand the small Clearwater store. Located as it was in the corner of a strip shopping center, expansion was only possible by extending the store out the back. The success of the original store was physically manifest in the 1984 augmentation, which quadrupled its original size and literally grafted a new, single-floor store building onto the rear façade of the existing shopping center.

After years of paying attention to the gentrifying Old Hyde Park neighborhood in Tampa, Jacobson's opened a one-story, forty-eight-thousand-square-foot store at 1501 West Swann Road in the historic neighborhood. "Tampa is a wonderfully cosmopolitan city," explained Mark K. Rosenfeld, Nathan's son, who had by the 1985 opening date become president and chief executive officer of Jacobson's. "A great number of people of discriminating taste live in the area, and we look forward to serving them," he said of the store that was, according to Jacobson's pre-opening press release, "subtly elegant and a new dimension in design."

The Tampa store, because of its neighborhood aspect, was closely related to its Michigan cousins and also became a favorite of nationally known celebrities. Store records indicate that Burt Reynolds, Shelly Fabares, Dorothy Hamill and even General Norman Schwarzkopf were served by Jacobson's obliging staff in Tampa.

Old Hyde Park neighborhood was the location for Jacobson's ninth Florida store. *Courtesy of the Ella Sharp Museum, Jackson, Michigan.*

Elaborate pen and magic-marker impression of Jacobson's in Naples, Florida, located in the Shops at Pelican Bay. *Courtesy of the Ella Sharp Museum, Jackson, Michigan.*

After years of legal wrangling, Jacobson's finally opened a store in Boca Raton in 1996. The design of the store hinted at the work of early Florida architect Addison Mizner. *Courtesy of the Ella Sharp Museum, Jackson, Michigan.*

Snowbird Store

In November 1992, Jacobson's opened a new store in Naples, Florida, in the Waterside Shops at Pelican Bay. Mary Glasgow, the store manager, had come from Jacobson's Dearborn store but had an interesting connection to Jacobson's past: she was a descendant of the owners of Glasgow's department store, an early Jacobson's competitor in Jackson, Michigan. Among many of her reminiscences of the store was an incident in which an older Florida resident didn't just drop her jaw while browsing in the store's sportswear shop; she also dropped her upper plate under a display, requiring the manager's expertise to retrieve it!

In its period of Florida expansion, Jacobson's penultimate store was an elaborate Classical structure in Boca Raton, once again on the state's east coast. Since 1988, the company expressed interest in locating a store in downtown's Mizner Plaza, but legal difficulties prevented it until late in 1996. Jacobson's fittingly opened its eighty-thousand-square-foot branch during the Christmas season with a gala entitled "An Evening with Dickens" benefitting the local Junior League.

Jacobson's growth in Florida served as a model for the company's future not just in its home state of Michigan but also across the Midwest as a regional luxury specialty department store with a fiercely loyal clientele.

Jacobson's Toledo store, shown from above, was approached from the mall through the store's characteristic heavy wooden entry doors. *Courtesy of Bill Garbe.*

Never on Sunday

We haven't found a mall we feel we belong in. We would consider going into one if the developers believe in the same merchandise principles we do, but none has so far.
—Russ Fowler, 1973

Nathan Rosenfeld loathed shopping malls. Until the early 1970s, Jacobson's always located its stores in the central business districts of the cities where it did business. The policy was no accident. No existing shopping mall, with its brash atmosphere, gimmicks and promotions, would enhance Jacobson's standing among its customers. In fact, according to Rosenfeld, it would be a step downward for his genteel, aristocratic store to attach itself to a mass-market shopping mall.

So it was with some trepidation that his executives proposed, in 1974, purchasing a vacant location of the Lamson Brothers Company, an old-line department store, in Toledo's Franklin Park Mall. History didn't record his exact words at the time, but Nathan Rosenfeld's refusal to consider the suggestion seemed firm: Jacobson's simply had no business in a mall. The Lamson location, no matter how attractive (a detailed analysis was prepared by advertising vice-president Fred Marx), would just have to sit there.

This story illustrates, again, the winning aspect of flexibility in Rosenfeld's leadership. The proponent of the Toledo plan asked Rosenfeld to join his team at lunch in the Terrace Room to hear their presentation, so, at the very least, they would not have to feel that they had wasted their time in

Jacobson's
FRANKLIN PARK

. . . now open, Talmadge at Sylvania, Toledo

Welcome to the beautiful new Jacobson's. . .a total fashion environment created for you, your family and home. On the first level, amid light, color and splendid surroundings, see complete selections of apparel and accessories for women, men and children from the world's most talented designers. On the second floor, delight in our decorative accents and gifts for the home, linens, skillfully crafted furnishings, and a helpful interior design studio. We're pleased to be here, part of a forward-thinking community with an exciting tempo of growth and development. You'll find us a good neighbor. . . dedicated to our tradition of integrity, quality and the courteous service for which we have been known for over 100 years. Come see us soon in our new Toledo home. We tried to think of everything to make shopping at Jacobson's a pleasant and satisfying experience.

OPEN 10 A.M. TO 6 P.M.
OPEN THURSDAY AND FRIDAY NIGHTS TO 9:30 P.M.
CLOSED SUNDAYS.
OPEN EVENINGS MONDAY THROUGH FRIDAY.
DURING THE HOLIDAY SEASON (STARTING NOV. 29)

Ad announcing Jacobson's arrival in the Toledo retail market in October 1974. The store normally did not take out full-page ads but made exceptions for important events such as the opening of a new store in a new city. *Courtesy of the Ella Sharp Museum, Jackson, Michigan.*

132

investigating the opportunity. After listening to their reasoning and taking the time to inquire about details, he enthusiastically announced, "I want you to buy that store as fast as you can!"

Several obstacles had to be overcome before Jacobson's could locate in Franklin Park Mall, which had been built by distinguished mall developer James Rouse. Jacobson's demanded an exemption from adhering to the mall's standard hours, meaning that it could maintain its own schedule and refrain from doing business on Sunday, a longstanding tradition. The store would also open only two nights per week, except during the holiday shopping period. Furthermore, it sought approval to install a pair of heavy wooden doors at its mall entrance, similar to those at its freestanding stores. "You should make an entrance into one of our stores, not feel as though you 'fell into it' from a mall," said Rosenfeld. The doors helped maintain Jacobson's cachet and set it apart from other stores, which he felt were inferior.

Rouse initially refused Jacobson's exceptions but, after meeting personally with Nathan Rosenfeld, agreed to the proposal *in toto*. He made it clear that he had been impressed by Rosenfeld's vision and came to see that the exemptions required by Jacobson's were well worth making in order to have such a fine anchor store in Franklin Park.

The ninety-thousand-square-foot store was redesigned, re-merchandised and re-staffed for its opening on October 23, 1974. Jacobson's store planning division, again under Keith Houck, took the slightly dowdy, three-year old Lamson's and transformed it into a typically handsome and home-like Jacobson's store. The transition was one of the most challenging, schedule-wise, ever presented to Houck's team and became known as the "nine-week wonder."

The tight schedule was not reflected in the quality of the store's completed interior design, described in opening day ads as "a total fashion environment…amid light, color, and splendid surroundings."

Local competitors Hudson's and Lasalle's featured designer apparel in their ads in the *Toledo Blade* on the same day, as if to try and counter the new store's impact. As soon as the next day, though, these competitors returned to their more promotional style of advertising, while Jacobson's continued in its own quiet, classic and inimitable style, eventually earning a valued position in the Toledo market.

Having satisfactorily entered a shopping mall, which it had resisted for so long, Jacobson's looked forward to strengthening its position in the Detroit market with a mall of its own making.

The new Great Oaks store presented a fresh, whitewashed face to the community, which waited patiently for the store to make its appearance in 1978. The copper canopies and coach lights adorned a store that was truly the epitome of a modern luxury retail facility. *Courtesy of the Ella Sharp Museum, Jackson, Michigan.*

Rochester, Bring the Car!

*When people own things, they feel they have a stake in society. When they owe
things, they may not have the same interest in preserving standards.*
—Nathan Rosenfeld

Even before Nathan Rosenfeld agreed to locate a store in Toledo's
Franklin Park Mall, he had, perhaps surprisingly, given serious
consideration to a shopping center location for Jacobson's. That is not to
say that he wasn't strong in his conviction that the average shopping center
wasn't a good place for his store. Rather, his plan was for Jacobson's to
create the shopping center in accordance with its own ideals, so it could
have a store in the prosperous town of Rochester, twenty-five miles due
north of Detroit. It became the fourth precious jewel in the necklace that
Jacobson's strung around the Motor City.

Jacobson's differed in its approach from other department stores, not
just regarding store location, as has already been seen, but in matters
of ownership as well. Again, the principle that Jacobson's was better off
owning its stores rather than leasing them was based on a deeply held belief
by Nathan Rosenfeld that ownership in itself had inherent value. Earlier,
when Jacobson's was still a small company lacking in the equity to purchase
or build the stores needed for expansion, he recognized that a developer
could leverage 100 percent of the cost of a project on the strength of a
lease from Jacobson's and soon began to question why Jacobson's couldn't
do the same thing for its own benefit. He believed that by owning his own
stores rather than leasing, he could pump the real estate profits back into

Russ Fowler, Judy Schaffer, Nathan Rosenfeld and store manager Phillip Culmone pose for a press shot outside the new Jacobson's store in Great Oaks. *Courtesy of the Ella Sharp Museum, Jackson, Michigan.*

the operations of the store and finance consistent improvements to the physical plant in order to keep Jacobson's fresh and up to date.

Many families who owned regional department stores split the ownership of the retail operations from the real estate entity that housed them. These companies failed over time as the real estate company profited from the lease payments but neglected to reinvest earnings to keep the operating companies competitive. Initially, Rosenfeld and his wife, Marjorie, formed the Summit Company to own Jacobson's real estate. Recognizing the inherent conflict that existed in other regional retailers and defying the conventional wisdom that a retailer couldn't (and shouldn't) invest valuable funds in its own physical plant, he merged the Summit Company into Jacobson's and formed a subsidiary, Jacobson Stores Realty Company, to own Jacobson's real estate. He was able to obtain favorable financing for construction projects based on the value of a Jacobson's lease and reinvest the tax savings gained from depreciation by uploading Jacobson Stores Realty's resulting cash flow to the operating parent. These investments

Jacobson's splendid interior at Great Oaks was more contemporary than that of the store's predecessors. Enriched with the work of local artists, it was, though, no less luxurious, as can be seen by the cosmetics department (top) and a view toward the Designer Salon (bottom). *Courtesy of the Ella Sharp Museum, Jackson, Michigan.*

fueled the growth of the company and set the foundation for Jacobson's eventual entry into the public equity markets in 1972.

In 1967, Jacobson's paid 32 percent of its lease costs to its own wholly owned subsidiary. Nine years later, that number had risen to 70 percent, as Rosenfeld put his philosophy into action.

Jacobson's Rochester story began when, in 1967, Jacobson Stores Realty Company purchased sixteen acres of land that was a part of a planned development, including a country club, condominiums, single-family residences and an office building. Jacobson's sought to execute the retail component of the complex, which was located on the corner of Walton Boulevard and Livernois Road and was known as Great Oaks. For many years, a sign on the property announcing that a Jacobson's store would open at the corner elicited constant questions about the project's status.

Seven years passed before Jacobson's began planning for the new store in earnest. It had waited patiently for the area's demographics to grow, along with the development of the adjacent property, until the store's construction became feasible. Jacobson's engaged Sam Frankel, a local developer, to create the fashion-oriented Great Oaks Mall, for which the seventy-thousand-square-foot Jacobson's store would serve as anchor.

The new store building itself presented a departure for Jacobson's. It was the first in Michigan to be joined to other complementary shops and restaurants in a climate-controlled environment. Aesthetically, it differed as well, with its masonry exterior this time bathed in a warm, off-white coat of paint. Copper canopies, traditional lanterns and brass nameplates, however, were incorporated as in the past, leaving no doubts about the store's heritage.

The premiere of Jacobson's Great Oaks on October 4, 1978, incorporated one of the store's long-held traditions. With every new opening, Jacobson's first honored contractors and their families with a reception in the store to thank them for their work, and afterward, a public preview would be held, also attended by store executives and local VIPs. The local *Rochester Eccentric* newspaper noted, somewhat surprisingly, that although the store was fully stocked and staffed for the evening, not a single piece of merchandise was sold. Phillip Culmone, who "graduated" to manager of the Rochester store from Grosse Pointe, explained, "We invited the public to drop by and get acquainted with Jacobson's, to see what we have without having to be concerned about prices."

Photographs taken at the event show a beaming Nathan Rosenfeld, by this time almost seventy-five years of age, greeting visitors amid the store's contemporary decor. The interior of the Rochester store, again the work of Jacobson's in-house planning department, certainly reflected a newer approach in its details, but the traditional warmth that characterized them was totally rooted in Jacobson's long-established culture. Locally sourced artwork was used prominently to decorate the interiors, and a central monumental staircase connected the store's two levels. In contrast to many common retail environments of the era, natural light spilled into the store through the large, arched windows integrated into the design and contributed to the store's home-like atmosphere.

Jacobson's Great Oaks store was a breakthrough project for the retailer. Jacobson's would go on to work again with another developer in order to create a second shopping center environment in Michigan and seek similar opportunities as it sought to take its Midwest presence beyond its home state's borders, to places that had never heard of it before.

Though it was created from a shell that was once home to Stewart's, the Louisville store's large-scale, arched entrances became an icon for Jacobson's. Its interior was spacious and elegant, very much like most new department stores of the 1990s. *Courtesy of the Ella Sharp Museum, Jackson, Michigan.*

Omnibus Jacobson's

A company makes a change in their management and says that this means they are converting to professional management instead of being managed by a family member. Nonsense. Professional is how much you know, what you do, and how well you do it.
—*Nathan Rosenfeld*

Nathan Rosenfeld celebrated his fortieth anniversary with Jacobson's in November 1979. At the time, he was showered with praise from his co-workers and employees. Each of the Jacobson's stores sent handmade cards, incorporating images of their respective stores, with signatures and well-wishes from their employees. He was honored once again at a testimonial dinner, and a follow-up letter from M.B. Townsend Jr., executive director of Jackson's Downtown Development Authority, thanked the merchant for his contributions to the city, saying that "they have not gone unnoticed and are very much appreciated. If we are to survive as a viable community, we need that kind of investment and spirit. It has always been a pleasure to work with you, Russ and Mark, and all of your other very capable executives whom I know share your enthusiasm and interest in the continued development of our city."

Almost three years later, on October 6, 1982, Jackson mayor Albert Stern declared Nathan Rosenfeld Day in honor of the retailer's "dedication and concern for the growth and development of the downtown area." Among the list of achievements for which he was lauded were the formation of a

Nathan and Marjorie share a moment on the newly remodeled second floor of the Jackson store on October 6, 1982, proclaimed by the city as Nathan Rosenfeld Day. Jackson Citizen-Patriot, 1982. *All rights reserved. Reprinted with permission.*

consortium to renovate Jackson's 1927 Hotel Hayes and his efforts to develop adequate parking in Jackson to support the vitality of the city's central business district. To mark the occasion, a reception was held in the Jackson store, whose second floor had just been renovated and was being dedicated as well. Just as in 1979, employees and well-wishers heaped praise on him with sincere appreciation for the accomplishments of his life's work.

Less than two months later, though, Rosenfeld was slowed by a struggle with cancer, but he managed to be at work at the store on the day after Thanksgiving. A few days later, he was admitted to Jackson's Foote Hospital West, where he passed away on Friday, December 3, 1982, having lived to the age of seventy-nine

The *Jackson Citizen-Patriot*, in its obituary, summarized the accomplishments of Michigan's great merchant, noting that annual sales of the store had been $300,000 in 1939, but by 1982, that figure had grown to over $181,262,000. Proudly, the newspaper listed the honors bestowed on him by the City of Jackson in 1959 for civic work, as well as similar honors from the City of Saginaw in 1977 and the Michigan State Chamber of Commerce in 1978.

Omnibus Jacobson's

After a Sunday funeral, Rosenfeld was laid to rest in Beth Israel Cemetery in Jackson. He and Marjorie just missed their fiftieth wedding anniversary, which they would have celebrated in June, had he lived.

The store acted quickly to fill the void left by Nathan Rosenfeld's death. After his older brother and business partner's untimely death in 1961, Rosenfeld served as chairman of the board with his trusted friend Russ Fowler as president. Meeting on the Monday after Rosenfeld's funeral, Jacobson's board of directors elected Fowler as chairman of the board and CEO and Mark Rosenfeld, Nathan's youngest son, as president of the 113-year-old company. With "a prince of a guy" (as Fowler was described) and a younger Rosenfeld, known as "as an optimist and kindhearted," leading Jacobson's, the sadness of Nathan Rosenfeld's absence was tinted with the light of optimism for the company's future.

The younger Rosenfeld had been familiar with his father's business and worked at various part-time jobs at Jacobson's during his youth. After serving as first lieutenant in the United States Army, Mark Rosenfeld, at the time twenty-six years of age, became a management trainee and served in

Portrait of Mark Rosenfeld, taken during the time of his presidency at Jacobson's. *Courtesy of the Ella Sharp Museum, Jackson, Michigan.*

Aerial impression of Laurel Park Place. Jacobson's is the structure in the lower left corner, attached to a shopping mall, hotel, parking deck and offices. *Courtesy of the Ella Sharp Museum, Jackson, Michigan.*

property management, buying and store management before being named to Jacobson's board of directors and eventually became executive vice-president in 1978. A graduate of Amherst College and the Massachusetts Institute of Technology, he was also an avid and accomplished tennis player, trained as a youth in the Hamtramck, Michigan tennis camp of coaching great Jean Hoxie.

He guided the store to record sales and earnings in 1985 and became chairman of the board in 1993, when Russ Fowler retired after forty-eight years with Jacobson's. Pam Schauffler, who reported directly to him, remembers Rosenfeld as being "a thoughtful and dedicated executive, who, though he didn't have the same charisma as his father, was effective in his own way, very consistent and accessible."

In the post–Nathan Rosenfeld era, Jacobson's continued its policy of renewing its stores, particularly in Ann Arbor, where a completely new "tapestry" brick façade endowed the building with a richer image. In the early 1980s, branch development was concentrated in Florida, but with the success of the 1978 Rochester store in Great Oaks Mall, Jacobson's partnered with a new developer to create Laurel Park Place, a multiuse complex in Livonia, Michigan, a western suburb of Detroit.

The 150,000-square-foot Livonia store opened on August 15, 1987, well before the rest of the complex, which followed eighteen months later. It

Pride and optimism aplenty at the grand opening of Jacobson's Livonia store. Among dignitaries, Russ Fowler is second from right; former Livonia mayor Edward H. McNamara stands to his left. *Courtesy of the Ella Sharp Museum, Jackson, Michigan.*

was the first in the chain to dispense with the time-honored tradition of hand-written sales slips and install a POS system. Eagerly anticipated, the large new branch was fairly stormed by customers after its ribbon-cutting ceremony. The POS system crashed, along with the store's air conditioning system, on the first day of business.

One entertaining anecdote from Livonia in Jacobson's later history is worth mentioning. In 1992, the store was the target of a lengthy strike by warehouse employees and delivery personnel. Unable to reach an agreement, the store began to replace two hundred employees before the Teamster's Local, which represented them, called off the strike. By this time, the workers who did not return voluntarily were forced to reapply for a position with the company. Disgruntled union members hoisted a banner in front of Laurel Park Place, which stated that "Jacobson's Peddles Pain & Suffering!" Not long after the banner went up, a well-heeled customer inquired, at one of the store's cosmetics counters, if she could get a sample of "Pain and Suffering," which she thought was the latest designer fragrance!

By the time Laurel Park Place opened, Jacobson's had announced that it would occupy a store in Indianapolis's Fashion Mall—Keystone at the Crossing—and in Columbus City Center, a new downtown mall in Ohio's state capital, developed by Alfred Taubman. By this time, Jacobson's aversion to shopping centers was a thing of the past. Coming into both new markets, Jacobson's still promised the quality merchandise and high-level service that had always been at the forefront of its traditions.

Understandably, the press in these locations wondered aloud about the newcomer. In an article entitled "What's a Jacobson's?" *Columbus Monthly* magazine prepared its readers for the arrival of the store by explaining what it found when visiting Jacobson's stores in Michigan. Both Russ Fowler and Mark Rosenfeld were quoted in the article, with Fowler stating that the store adhered strongly to its principles of quality and service because "it's difficult to serve a gourmet dinner through a vending machine." A contemporary article in *Chicago Apparel News*, with some bewilderment, described the Jacobson's customer as a shopper who "would rather *not* shop than switch to another store." Mark Rosenfeld himself echoed the sentiments of his father about the store's refusal to engage in price promotion, saying, "The credibility of our store is the most important asset we have. What we *do* do, however, is promote fashion, timelessness, service and value."

The 120,000-square-foot Indianapolis store opened in 1989, with the smaller, 114,000-square-foot Columbus store following it with tremendous acclaim in August 1989. After years of downtown decline, residents

A simple sketch illustrates the new 1988 Sargent Road headquarters of Jacobson's. *Courtesy of the Ella Sharp Museum, Jackson, Michigan.*

The good results from the new Briarwood store presaged the success Jacobson's was to find in mall locations across the Midwest. *Courtesy of the Ella Sharp Museum, Jackson, Michigan.*

and businesses in Columbus were overjoyed to see such a positive retail development in the center of their city, and Jacobson's presence there was like icing on the cake.

Also in 1988, Jacobson's moved to a new headquarters and distribution center, located northeast of Jackson, neatly overlooking Brills Lake. Attractive and rural as it was, the site was also chosen for the excellent and visible access it had to Interstate 94, which connected many of the company's stores. At the time of its dedication, news reports described the fairly high cost and impressive features of the building, but the store consciously kept its new headquarters low key so as not to mislead vendors, consultants or investors into thinking that the company was overly extravagant. It had, in fact, enjoyed another profitable year in 1986, but the cost of expansion into new markets and new technology would have to be absorbed by upcoming years' bottom lines.

Even in 1988, retail and business analysts, while agreeing that Jacobson's was a well-run, first-class company, soured on the store's conservative policies, such as staying closed on Sunday. Also criticized was the company's refusal to raise interest rates on credit cards to the maximum allowed by law.

As president, Mark Rosenfeld followed in his father's footsteps by addressing a perennial problem faced by Jacobson's: parking near its downtown locations. Articles in the *Ann Arbor News* illustrate the struggle facing Ann Arbor's downtown. Citing both security and maintenance issues in the store's adjacent Maynard Street parking deck, Rosenfeld stated frankly in May 1990 that the store was considering leaving downtown, explaining that "it's been a good store, but the trend for us in the last few years hasn't been very positive." The situation was exacerbated by crime in the area, including several assaults and robberies on Jacobson's corner and a fight in the garage that left one man dead. Store employees became accustomed to customers hauling in chunks of concrete that had fallen from the neglected parking structure.

It came as no surprise when, after what the store saw as inadequate action by the city regarding parking and security, Jacobson's announced that it would close the downtown store it had operated since 1924 and relocate to a vacant former Lord & Taylor store in Briarwood Mall to the south. The location was never successful for the New York retailer, and for a number of years, it offered the store to Jacobson's. Sentimental toward downtown, Rosenfeld resisted, until Lord & Taylor literally begged Jacobson's to take the space, dropping its initial price by over 80 percent. It was an offer that the store couldn't refuse, especially when the city wasn't willing to make the investments necessary to keep it downtown.

After a major reconstruction, the Briarwood Jacobson's opened in October 1993 and became one of the company's most successful stores. By this time in the company's history, its downtown locations must have begun to seem as anachronistic as its Sunday policy, which was dropped in 1991, when the stores began regular Sunday hours.

In spite of these bumps in the road, Jacobson's was able to post record sales gains in the early 1990s. It opened branches in new markets, first adding a store in November 1994 in Louisville, Kentucky's existing Oxmoor Center. A major remodeling of a 156,000-square-foot building once occupied by Stewart's, Louisville's most well-regarded department store, gave Jacobson's a foothold in a new market, which it needed as the economy in its home state of Michigan stagnated.

In fact, Jacobson's strategy of expanding into new markets caused it to look at acquisitions as well. The store examined the possibility of purchasing retailers with similar cachet in growing markets. Neusteter's of Denver and Frost Bros. in San Antonio were considered, but their reliance on leases made them poor matches for Jacobson's. Sakowitz, located in Houston and once considered a rival to Neiman-Marcus, was similarly rejected. Later, Jacobson's looked at California's well-loved I. Magnin & Co., but it

Omnibus Jacobson's

The elegant Jacobson's store in Leawood, a suburb of Kansas City, perfectly expressed the optimism of the store as it explored new places of business. *Courtesy of the Ella Sharp Museum, Jackson, Michigan.*

ultimately decided to pursue a strategy of opening branches in new markets instead of mergers.

In 1996, Jacobson's debuted in the Towne Center, an upscale development in the southern Kansas City suburb of Leawood. Both the Louisville and Kansas City stores were based on the Briarwood model and reflected contemporary retail design of the day, with blank exterior walls and large, arched entryways with covered, sky-lit canopies to assist customers arriving by car. The interiors were likewise, sleek and sky lit, composed of elegant materials and full of enticingly displayed merchandise.

Yet for all their forward thinking, the stores' very departure from tradition in significant ways signaled that Jacobson's itself was changing. Whether customers welcomed the change didn't have to be questioned at the time; mall shopping on Sundays and electronic cash registers had become as much a norm in the 1990s as white gloves and a trip downtown had been in Nathan Rosenfeld's day. Yet the store found itself in financial difficulties by the mid-1990s as Michigan's economy crumbled.

In spite of an attempt to woo younger customers and explore new markets, Jacobson's experienced static sales growth, a drop in its stock price from a high of $26 per share in 1990 to $8 by 1995 and a $4.2 million loss. In November 1996, it announced that Mark Rosenfeld was retiring, and a press release stated, "We deeply appreciate the leadership, friendship, and commitment to the company's traditions which Mark has demonstrated during his 24-

149

year career at Jacobson's." It was widely accepted that the move had been in the works for some time. To insiders and employees, though, the perception was different: Mark Rosenfeld had been forced out, "taking the fall" for the store's slide into the red, according to some, or capitulating to a disgruntled board that had already decided on his replacement.

That replacement was P. Gerald Mills, a veteran retail executive who had been coaxed out of retirement to take the Jacobson post. The sixty-eight-year-old Mills started his career at L.S. Ayres in Indianapolis and was instrumental in developing that store's Ayr-Way discount division. He was also familiar in Detroit as chairman and CEO of the Dayton-Hudson Corp. since 1978 and later with Hudson's, from 1981 to 1985. In this capacity, he presided over the difficult shutdown of Hudson's landmark Woodward Avenue store.

Within a year of Mills's appointment, Jacobson's announced that it was closing unprofitable stores in the downtowns of Jackson, Kalamazoo and Dearborn. It dropped its furniture business and its bridal salons, consolidated the Store for the Home operations into the main buildings in remaining locations and became more price-promotional. The extensive list of longtime employees who resigned or retired from Jacobson's at the time read like a who's who of the store's history. Mark Rosenfeld remained on the board until 1998, remembering that "there really wasn't any reason to stay, but I did remain the largest single shareholder."

In 2000, Jacobson's announced that the East Lansing store would close with the opening of a new facility in Meridian Mall in Okemos. Jacobson's also touted its new, smaller specialty store format, which it unveiled in 2001, when it closed the well-established Longwood store in Florida and moved to a sixty-thousand-square-foot space in the Renaissance Centre, a strip mall next to the Altamonte Mall in suburban Orlando. Located in a difficult corner position, it was not the sensation the store had hoped for and produced lackluster results during its short lifetime.

The drastic cost-cutting measures implemented after Mark Rosenfeld's departure improved the store's bottom line, but the Jacobson's that generations of Michiganians (and Floridians) knew was clearly a thing of the past, and its horizons were anything but bright.

We All Fall Down

Unless we take care of ourselves, we all go to pot. And if we have a business, and we don't take care of it...if all we're doing is trying to get an immediate profit... then our business goes to pot.
—Nathan Rosenfeld

Jacobson's 1999 annual report, entitled *Success Is Taking Shape*, is a fairly optimistic document. The commentary provided by the store's management outlined a bright future for Jacobson's, based on the changes put in place in the post-Rosenfeld years. Numbers, shown in the report, confirm that the store had turned away from a devastating $11.5 million loss in 1996 and produced small profits of over $1 million in the next two years. The year 1999 saw the profit more than double to $3.5 million.

The report also mentions that the store had launched a presence on the World Wide Web and was studying the application of e-commerce at Jacobson's as well. New stores were planned in Okemos, Michigan, to replace the established East Lansing store in 2000, and in Altamonte, Florida, to replace the Longwood store in 2001. By this time, East Lansing had gained a reputation as a rowdy college town, occasionally prone to rioting centered on university sports–related incidents. Long past was the era in which a Jacobson's store fit into a town like East Lansing; the controlled environment of a mall was now seen as the best location for the company's specialty store format.

Employees and customers still saw Jacobson's as a positive part of the retail environment. To attract younger customers, the store changed the name of its well-known Miss J shop first to Ms. J and then to Che Bella! (Italian for "How Beautiful!") to attract a more sophisticated customer. Its Custom Size Shop was renamed Clairewood in an attempt to corner the growing market for larger-size clothing. The full-service restaurants were, for the most part, removed, but a modern Jake's Café in many of the branches served the customer's need for a place to get refreshment while shopping. The environment in some stores was remodeled in the style of Jacobson's successful new stores in Ann Arbor and Louisville.

To some customers, however, and to the employees who served them, the store was losing the Jacobson's magic. It became more promotional, while the price points of the merchandise grew toward the upper end of the scale, putting some customers off. As Nathan Rosenfeld had predicted, this caused the store to lose credibility when the same merchandise could be had for less at off-price retailers—at least in theory. While Jacobson's had always had a reputation as a "carriage trade" store, in the past, insiders knew that it offered value for high-quality merchandise and that its assortments were often rounded out by moderately priced items for those with thinner wallets.

The new look of the stores, while attractive, was similar to what other retailers were doing, again blurring the distinction between Jacobson's and its competition. At stores that didn't receive a total makeover, the environment declined fairly severely, making them seem, at least to some degree, as promotional as the discounters that had been taking away the company's business.

Jacobson's 1999 annual report touted the retailer's new store in Okemos, Michigan's Meridian Mall, which would replace its fifty-nine-year presence in East Lansing. *Courtesy of the Ella Sharp Museum, Jackson, Michigan.*

We All Fall Down

In June 2001, the seventy-six-year-old Gerald Mills, who led the company since late 1996, relinquished the chief executive officer and president's positions he held to Carol Williams, an executive from Saks Department Stores, at the time headquartered in Birmingham, Alabama. The announcement of Williams's appointment noted her "vision, taste and financial skills" as key to Jacobson's transformation as a high-end specialty retailer. She was Jacobson's first female president, in some way carrying on a tradition at a company that valued its female employees. With the Williams appointment, Mills went back into retirement, which had been his goal for some time.

In spite of a new CEO and some new store locations, Jacobson's continued to lose market share. Retailers like Neiman-Marcus, Parisian and Nordstrom had moved into the Detroit area and became established with customers at the same time that Jacobson's was trying to define what its future should be. The loyal, treasured Jacobson's customer, the one who'd rather not shop than switch, was a thing of the past. In 2000, the country was in the waning years of the dot-com boom; the economy in Michigan, however, flirted with disaster, and not surprisingly, the Florida stores readily outperformed the Michigan ones. Losses for the year totaled $2.8 million.

Then came 9/11. The store, foundering, was itself overstocked at the very top with fine jewelry and designer couture—things customers in a shocked nation could not and would not buy. The losses for 2001 amounted to a staggering $57 million. Jacobson's began defaulting on its obligations in November 2001 and filed for bankruptcy protection on January 15, 2002.

At the time of the filing, Jacobson's had secured a $130 million interim loan to carry it through a restructuring period and planned to close its stores in Clearwater, Osprey, Tampa, Toledo and Columbus as a cost-saving move. Trading in Jacobson's stock was suspended with the bankruptcy filing, but by March, Jacobson Stores, Inc., was de-listed by Nasdaq; it could not meet the requirements for continued listing on the stock exchange. Its stock had sunk to forty-six cents.

In May 2002, the company revealed its plans for reorganization. It hired Financo, Inc., a New York investment banker, to help with the reorganization by finding new investors to supply cash and to seek a suitor who would purchase the company whole, thereby keeping it intact. At the time of the announcement of the Financo deal, president Carol Williams said that the losses of the past were "old news," but while speaking with optimism about Jacobson's most recent performance, she failed to provide any specific positive data.

None of it was meant to be. By the end of June, Jacobson's admitted that the grievous losses were mounting, and "not a single bidder" had emerged to purchase the company intact. Instead, the company asked the bankruptcy court to open bids in July from parties interested in Jacobson's headquarters, its other real estate, its credit card receivables and even its trademark name. At the end of July, to the horror of its twenty-eight hundred employees, Jacobson's asked the bankruptcy court for permission to liquidate. Federal bankruptcy judge David T. Stosberg announced, "Jacobson's is going to close. Nobody's happy about it, but the time has come."

Accordingly, "closing" banners went up and the liquidation sales began. Some controversy occurred over the revelation that the liquidators were selling merchandise from other outlets during the sale, and customers complained that some prices were actually better before the liquidation began. Not a lot of this mattered for Jacobson's salespeople, who struggled to maintain the level of service for which they had been trained; even at that, employees noted that "Jacobson's customers" had long ago abandoned the store. Going-out-of-business-sale customers were bargain hunters and the curious who wanted to see "what happened" to the once-great store.

By September 15, the stores had liquidated, and employees were relieved of their positions. Almost immediately, postmortems appeared in the press. Notably, Mark Rosenfeld, who had remained on Jacobson's board of directors until 1998 and whose remaining stock in the company had been canceled, stated that, in hindsight, he "probably should have fought" his 1996 ouster from the company built by his father.

Similarly, Jim Delaney, former vice-president of human resources, remembers the final dark days of Jacobson's. He recalls a discussion with a court-appointed bankruptcy consultant who openly bragged that "there is a lot of money to be made on bankruptcies like this." When the same individual left his interim office, whistling cheerfully down the corridor past Delaney, the Jacobson's veteran went into the CEO's office and said, "Carol, we're screwed."

A magnificent bit of ephemera: a sales slip from Jacobson's glory days, when all receipts were handwritten. *Courtesy of Bill Garbe*

154

We All Fall Down

In fact, many like Delaney don't agree that Jacobson's had no choice but to liquidate. The Mills regime had replaced practically every store manager and a great deal of the headquarters leadership with its own people. After years of struggling, many were ready to throw in the towel. The force of history and the presence of Nathan Rosenfeld, that most principled of businessmen, had moved on, leaving a spiritual vacuum that ensured that the only finale would be bankruptcy and closure.

In fact, mentioning the name of Nathan Rosenfeld helps bring the Jacobson's story full circle to a conclusion. Or does it? Jim Zuleski, who served for many years with the company in Florida and Michigan, mused about what might have happened had Nathan Rosenfeld been granted more years to lead his company: "He would have had a heck of a time. He was a headstrong leader, and the world changed, leaving some of his most deeply held beliefs about retailing fairly anachronistic. He would have had trouble changing with the times." Yet others, like Linda Salah, who locked the doors of the Great Oaks store for the last time in September 2002, disagree. She believes that "Mark's dad was an incredibly astute businessman who would have known what to do to save his beloved store."

True or not, the final effect was the same for the store, the employees and its customers. A void was created. An institution associated with the state of Michigan (and to a lesser degree, Florida) had virtually disappeared. The communities in which Jacobson's flourished had lost an excellent employer, a good neighbor and a place where many, many memories were created. Worst of all, the central business districts of these cities lost their best advocate in the private sector, which is to say they lost their best advocate, period.

While it seems obvious to say that time bypassed Jacobson's, when possible alternate explanations for the store's demise are explored, puzzling questions arise: Did time indeed pass it by, or did the Jacobson's of Nathan Rosenfeld, great merchant, pass time by long ago? Were his hallowed principles, and the will to adhere to them (with spectacular results), a thing too good for today's retail culture and the society of which it is a component? Did Jacobson's deteriorate in the face of a changing American retail scene, or did the scene deteriorate so badly that a store as genuinely good, valuable and decent as Jacobson's could not hope to endure in it? Was the demise all about Jacobson's, or was it really about us?

The answer to these questions must remain, sadly, a case of speculation, no matter how clear hindsight might seem to be. The answer is every bit as perplexing as the countess's dilemma in the opera *Capriccio* discussed at the opening of this book.

"Dinner is served!"

The Jackson Cortland Room restaurant and The Top of the Fountain in Dearborn were typical of Jacobson's well-regarded restaurants. Both are shown as they appeared when new. *Courtesy of the Ella Sharp Museum, Jackson, Michigan.*

Let's Do Lunch

You don't have to have everything, but whatever you do have, be the best in.
—Nathan Rosenfeld

As a retail establishment, Jacobson's desired to be a welcoming host to its customers, but its restaurant operations were actually born of necessity at the central office in the late 1940s. The relocation of employees from the store's former offices in downtown Jackson to a rural site outside the city devoid of amenities brought up questions about where they would eat lunch. The already-mentioned employee cafeteria was programmed into the original CD building. Known as the Terrace Room, it was consistently enlarged and improved.

Jacobson's benevolent attitude toward its employees resulted in good employee dining facilities in most of its stores, but the concept of a restaurant for customers didn't come to reality until 1957, when the St. Clair Room opened on the lower level of the Grosse Pointe store. The dining room became a popular rendezvous for shoppers in the Village and helped make Jacobson's a focal point of the district. When the store went through its major transformation in 1974, a new space for the St. Clair Room was found at the back of the first floor. French doors allowed the handsome, Colonial-style room to spill out onto the gardens of D'Hondt Way, a real plus during the short season of pleasant summer weather in Michigan.

In addition to providing refreshment to customers, the St. Clair Room, as well as the rest of Jacobson's restaurants, served as an event venue for fashion shows, special events receptions and employee recognition dinners, most often held after store closing times.

When Jacobson's built its new Jackson store in 1961, the adjacent Dowsett Building was acquired in order to accommodate a restaurant on the ground floor. The Cortland Room, so named because it was located on the side of the building facing Cortland Street, was a success from the start and helped establish a reputation for hospitality for Jacobson's.

Though it competed with rival L.H. Field's Rose Room, the Cortland Room was a favorite dining spot in downtown Jackson, well patronized by employees from the large Consumer's Power headquarters located on the other side of Michigan Avenue. Detroit-area Consumer's Energy employees Bobbie Frezell and Al Orosco recall attending training sessions at their employer's Jackson head office and walking over to the Cortland Room on lunch hour. "It was our favorite place to eat in Jackson," says Frezell. "The food was always good, and it was a real treat to go there." Orosco adds, "Knowing that we'd go there for lunch made the training sessions go by faster! I especially liked the Hungarian Mushroom Soup."

The deluxe building erected for Jacobson's Dearborn store in 1964 had a lovely and deservedly popular dining room on the second floor named the Top of the Fountain. Located next to the store's unique spiral staircase with a cascading fountain bubbling in its center, the bright room featured large, curtained windows overlooking the Michigan Avenue shopping scene below. The Top of the Fountain was the first time a new Jacobson's store had an integral dining facility from its inception.

While these restaurants could be classed as above-average department store tearooms, the 1970 East Room, in Jacobson's new, from-the-ground-up East Lansing store, sought to extend the hand of the store's hospitality offerings further. The large, wide-windowed dining room, located atop the store and decorated with elaborate Asian-influenced furniture, was also accessible via an upper-level bridge from the adjacent parking deck. As a result, it offered dinner on the nights that the store was closed. In its style, location and presentation of excellent gastronomic offerings, the East Room became justifiably popular and is still spoken of positively today. In addition to culinary excellence, it is remembered for the lovely, sweeping treetop panorama of the Michigan State University campus across East Grand River Avenue.

Jacobson's ambitious "superblock" project in Saginaw housed two restaurants. One, a multiroom complex with a club-like bar, was leased to Detroit restaurateur Machus Enterprises. The chain of restaurants was founded as a bakery in 1933 by Harris Machus and grew to eight locations, from the original cafeteria and bakery in Birmingham to the luxurious but notorious Machus Red Fox, known for the disappearance of former teamster president Jimmy Hoffa in 1975. The Saginaw restaurant was named Machus Sly Fox and, like other Machus restaurants, was famous for its Machus salad with Roquefort cheese and crumbled bacon and its excellent baked goods.

The second restaurant in Saginaw was called Le Buffet and was operated by Jacobson's. It featured an old-fashioned ice cream parlor and more tearoom fare.

After Jacobson's in Kalamazoo was remodeled in the late 1970s, a restaurant on the third floor was added to the store's offerings. Called the Garden Spot, it was small compared to the store's other restaurants but became, like the rest of them, a popular and admired place to eat and socialize in downtown Kalamazoo.

With its later expansion, Jacobson's incorporated small Jake's Cafés in its stores. Surprisingly, the Birmingham store, despite its status as a flagship due to its size, did not have a restaurant, although an adjoining Peter Pan restaurant took orders from Jacobson's beauty salon next door for delivery to patrons there. The Birmingham store did have, however, a large employee dining room and, in later years, opened a Jake's Café for customers on its lower level, at the bottom of the apparel store's spiral staircase.

The store's restaurant menus offered a wide range of tempting food and were rounded out by daily specials and seasonal favorites. On the evenings when the store was open, a dinner buffet was served and became a popular event for families who shopped together. Traditional fashion shows and holiday events like Breakfast with Santa all added to the warmth and conviviality of this most gracious of retail institutions. The following recipes are from Jacobson's archives, adapted and tested by the author.

JACOBSON'S CHEESE SOUP

½ cup diced carrot
½ cup diced celery
¼ teaspoon white pepper
1 stick butter
¼ cup plus 1 tablespoon flour
6 cups water
6 teaspoons chicken base
1 pound American cheese, cut in cubes
½ cup half and half, warmed
Cayenne pepper to taste

Sauté carrot, celery and white pepper in ¼ stick of butter in a frying pan. Remove carrot and celery and set aside. Melt ¾ stick of butter. Over heat, whisk flour into butter to form a roux. Set aside.

Boil water in a large stock pot. Add chicken base and sautéed vegetables. Bring to a boil; simmer for 10 minutes. Slowly add cheese cubes, whisking until melted. When cheese is melted, whisk in roux in small batches, adding slowly to avoid lumps. Allow soup to cook for 10 to 15 minutes, until thickened. Remove from heat and add heated half and half. Season with cayenne pepper, if desired. Makes about four servings.

JACOBSON'S MING DYNASTY CASSEROLE

1 can sliced water chestnuts, chopped
1 can chow mein noodles
1 can cream of mushroom soup
1 cup diced celery
1 can chunk-style tuna, drained
¼ pound cashew pieces
¼ cup onion, minced
Pepper to taste

Mix all ingredients, holding ¼ cup noodles for the top. Spoon into a greased casserole dish and sprinkle reserved noodles over top. Bake at 325 degrees for 40 minutes.

JACOBSON'S CASHEW CHICKEN SALAD

1 pound cooked chicken
¼ cup diced celery
¼ cup chopped green onion
2 tablespoons raisins
¼ cup cashew pieces

Dressing

2 tablespoons mango chutney
¾ cup mayonnaise
¼ teaspoon curry powder

Combine chicken, celery, chopped green onion, raisins and cashews. Purée mango chutney and add to mayonnaise. Season with curry powder. Combine with chicken mixture and allow to cool in the refrigerator for 2 hours before serving.

JACOBSON'S QUICHE LORRAINE

6 large eggs
½ cup half and half, mixed with ½ cup 2 percent milk
1½ cup shredded cheddar cheese
1½ cup shredded Swiss (Emmental) cheese
1 large pie shell
½ teaspoon dry basil
Paprika
Nutmeg

Beat eggs slightly. Add half and half and milk and beat again. Place shredded cheese into pie shell. Add basil to eggs and milk and pour over cheese in the pie shell. Dust the top of the pie shell with paprika and nutmeg. Place quiche on a baking sheet lined with parchment paper. Bake at 325 degrees for 40 to 45 minutes. Quiche is done when a knife poked into the center comes out clean. Let cool for 10 minutes and cut into 8 slices.

Jacobson's

Appetizers

Jacobson's own Cheese Soup .... Cup 2.00 Bowl 2.65
A rich and creamy soup topped with croutons.

Soup of the Day .... Cup 1.85 Bowl 2.40

Chilled Fruit Cup 1.75

Croissant 1.95

Muffin *Baked fresh daily. (Ask about our low fat muffins)* 1.00

French Fried Potatoes 1.55

Ask your server about our Chef's Creation for today.

Salads

Add a Cup of Soup for 1.45 when you purchase any Entree Salad.

Chicken Caesar Salad 7.25
Crisp Romaine lettuce, croutons and Caesar style dressing, topped with strips of tender, grilled chicken breast. Accompanied by muffin or roll, and butter.

Chicken or Tuna Salad 5.95
White meat chicken or tuna, blended with mayonnaise, celery, and spices. Served on a bed of lettuce with hard cooked egg wedges. Accompanied by muffin or roll and butter, and fresh fruit.

Maurice Salad 6.75
Crisp lettuce, julienne strips of ham, turkey and Swiss cheese, served with our special dressing. Accompanied by muffin or roll, and butter.   Small 5.75

Grilled Chicken and Pasta Salad 6.25
Slices of tender and juicy chicken breast served over rotini pasta and vegetables, tossed in our parmesan italian dressing and sprinkled with crumbles of feta cheese. Accompanied by muffin or roll, and butter.

Fisherman's Salad 6.75
A blend of Pacific white fish and crab meat, celery, almonds, and a tangy dressing, served on a bed of crisp lettuce. Accompanied by muffin or roll, and butter.   Small 5.75

Side Salad 1.95

Dressings:
Buttermilk, Parmesan, Italian, Maurice, Caesar, Celery Seed, Raspberry Vinegarette and Honey Mustard

Beverages

Gourmet Coffee *Ask your server about today's fresh brewed flavor.* 1.35

Regular or decaffeinated Coffee, Hot Tea, or Milk .... .85

Coca Cola, or Assorted Soft Drinks. *Complimentary refills.* .... .90

TŶ NANT *Still Spring Water, in the blue bottle. Imported from Bethania, Wales.* 1.95

Children's menu available for those 10 years old and under.

06/95U/A

A Cortland Room menu dating from 1995. In addition to this card, specials on this day included seafood quesadilla, rotollo florentine, pot roast, crab cakes and pasta giordano. Lighter specials offered were grilled eggplant foccacia, smoked turkey focaccia, smoked turkey rueben, caesar in a pita and stacked lawash sandwich. *Courtesy of the Ella Sharp Museum, Jackson, Michigan.*

162

Sandwiches

Add a Cup of Soup for 1.45 when you purchase any Sandwich.

Croissant Melt 6.25
*A flaky croissant topped with wafered turkey and ham, asparagus spears, melted
Monterey Jack cheese, lettuce, tomato and honey mustard dressing.*

Grilled Chicken Breast 5.25
*A tender and juicy skinless chicken breast on a multi-grain bun with lettuce,
tomato, honey mustard and our carrot and black-eyed pea relish.*

Soup and a Half 5.75
*A cup of soup and one half of a Chunky Chicken Salad or Tuna Salad sandwich,
served with tomato slices and lettuce.*

Beefburger 4.75
*Six ounces of lean ground beef, cooked to your taste and served on a Kaiser roll
with lettuce, tomato, onion and our special carrot and black-eyed pea relish.* **With cheese ..** 4.95

Jacobson's Club... 5.75
*A triple-decker with turkey, bacon, mayonnaise, lettuce and tomato, on your
choice of bread.*

Meatloaf Sandwich 4.95
Slices of juicy meatloaf served hot or cold on your choice of bread.

Hot Turkey Sandwich 5.25
*Sliced breast of turkey on your choice of bread, served with mashed potatoes
and gravy.*

Chicken or Tuna Salad Sandwich 5.25
Served with crisp lettuce and tomato slices on your choice of bread or croissant.

(Above sandwiches served with potato chips)

Entrees

Add a Cup of Soup for 1.45 when you purchase any Entree.

Quiche Lorraine 6.50
*Our version of the French classic. Eggs, bacon, and cheese baked in a
pastry shell. Served with a fruit cup, muffin and our special carrot and
black-eyed pea relish.*

Quiche of the Day... 6.50
*A special quiche prepared daily and served with a fruit cup, muffin and carrot
and black-eyed pea relish.*

Meatloaf 6.95
*Lean Ground beef and served hot with whipped potatoes, gravy,
vegetable and a crisp tossed salad.*

Chicken Pot Pie 6.75
*White meat chicken, vegetables, creamy gravy and flaky puff pastry, served with
a crisp tossed salad.*

For your convenience you may use your Jacobson's charge card, MasterCard, Visa or American Express card.

06/95L/B

Jacobson's also prided itself on desserts. On the day this menu was served, a dessert card was included that featured fruits of the forest pie, French silk pie, New York cheesecake with strawberries, sundaes, milkshakes and a well-remembered specialty, "Jacobson's own" bread pudding. An attachment to the dessert card proffered "our latest finds—scrumptious new desserts to tempt your palate." *Courtesy of the Ella Sharp Museum, Jackson, Michigan.*

JACOBSON'S HUNGARIAN MUSHROOM SOUP

¼ pound butter
4 medium onions, sliced thinly
2½ pounds fresh white mushrooms, cleaned and sliced
1 tablespoon dill weed
1 tablespoon sweet paprika
4 mushroom bullion cubes
12 cups water
¾ cup warm water
½ cup flour
1 12-ounce container sour cream, thinned with milk

Melt butter in the bottom of a large stockpot. Add onions, mushrooms, dill weed and paprika. Sauté until the onions are translucent. Dissolve mushroom bullion in water and add to sautéed mixture. Bring to a boil and simmer for 30 minutes. Mix warm water and flour into a thin paste. Return soup to a boil, add flour paste in a thin stream and simmer for 10 to 15 minutes, until thickened. Remove from heat. Temper sour cream and milk mixture by slowly adding a ladle of soup to the cream. Slowly mix sour cream into the soup and serve. Do not boil when reheating.

JACOBSON'S GARDEN SANDWICH

2 green onions
4 medium-size fresh white mushrooms, sliced
1 tablespoon butter
1 small package frozen spinach, thawed and chopped
Lemon juice and pepper to taste
4 slices each medium cheddar cheese, provolone and Swiss
8 slices light rye bread

Lightly sauté onions and mushrooms in butter. Add thawed spinach and heat through. Season with lemon juice and pepper. Assemble sandwiches starting with provolone and cheddar cheeses. Spread a layer of spinach mixture on top of cheese and top with Swiss. Grill sandwiches as for grilled cheese or heat in sandwich press.

JACOBSON'S FISHERMAN'S SALAD

Salad Mixture

¾ pound deli imitation crab sticks, shredded (or use cooked lump crabmeat)
½ cup diced celery
¼ cup chopped green onion
2 tablespoons toasted sliced almonds
¼ teaspoon dill weed

Dressing

½ cup mayonnaise
¼ cup grated Parmesan cheese
¼ cup milk
1½ teaspoons minced garlic
1 teaspoon dried parsley
½ teaspoon fresh lemon juice

Whisk all items together and cool in refrigerator for at least 1 hour.

Assembly

4 large leaves head lettuce, shredded into ¼-inch shreds
2 vine tomatoes, quartered into wedges
2 hard-boiled eggs, quartered into wedges
12 pitted Kalamata olives

Combine crab sticks, celery, onion, almonds and dill weed with dressing, reserving some dressing for final presentation.

Line bowls with lettuce strips. Place a scoop of seafood mixture on lettuce in each bowl. Place a tomato wedge at 12 and 6 o'clock near the rim of the bowl. Place an egg wedge at 3 and 9 o'clock near the rim of the bowl. Place 3 olives on top center of salad scoop to decorate. Serve with additional dressing on the side.

Finding Jacobson's

The discerning public is learning that discount stores sell only discount goods at discount prices. These customers will continue to favor stores with integrity, which sell legitimate merchandise and give good customer service.
—Nathan Rosenfeld

To say that Jacobson's left a vacuum when it closed would be an understatement. The store's demise could be traced back over a long period, but it became painfully clear that a familiar bit of Michigan—and to a degree, Florida—disappeared forever when the doors closed for the last time. The store that provided an alternative to typical retail, with its downtown locations, lush interiors, courtly salespeople and distinctively edited merchandise, was, quite simply, gone for good.

In its place were vacant buildings, and when the temporary "going out of business" signs came down, so did the familiar Jacobson's name, which had graced these structures for decades. Announcements were soon made that Jacobson's mall properties, for the most part, were sold to competitors who coveted their locations.

Of these, the most interesting to customers in mourning for Jake's was Von Maur, a Davenport, Iowa retailer. Known throughout most of its history as Petersen's, Petersen Harned Von Maur had taken a new name in 1989, after closing its historical flagship store and becoming a fashion-oriented specialty store, branching successfully into new markets. Jacobson's traditional customers could be forgiven for thinking that the Iowa firm would be "the new Jacobson's." News reports at the time compared the store favorably with Jacobson's. It fit the mold promisingly enough, featuring edited collections of better fashion apparel and focusing on customer service. From the start, though, Von Maur made it clear that it was only interested in the Briarwood and Laurel Park locations in Michigan. While the store's entry into parts of Jacobson's former market was welcomed, the news would mean nothing to the remaining cities for which Jacobson's had been a downtown anchor.

Von Maur ultimately occupied the Louisville store opened in 1996, gaining a spot in that city's popular Oxmoor Center shopping mall.

Some of Jacobson's other locations were taken by more familiar retailers. Younker's, another Iowa name that was, at the time, owned by the Saks Department Store Group, moved into the Meridian Mall location in Okemos, Michigan. Such was the quality of the environment that Younker's inherited that virtually no improvements had to be made in order for it to conduct business. Macy's moved into the Kansas City store, while Saks Fifth Avenue took over the Indianapolis branch.

Jacobson's Toledo store was demolished for an expansion of Franklin Park Mall, which resulted in a new mall wing and a Dillard's store in place of the original Lamson Brothers Building that Jake's had purchased in 1974. The Columbus City Center location was also eventually demolished, but the story in that location was less upbeat. The mall declined drastically, while multiple new shopping centers were built in the more affluent neighborhoods on the north side of the city, stripping the once-vibrant and attractive mall of its customers. A gang-related slaying in the mall in 1994 raised questions about the viability of retail in Columbus's downtown. Eventually, not only Jacobson's, but also the handsome branch of Marshall Field & Company, was demolished, along with the rest of the urban mall's tenant space. Even the beloved downtown Lazarus store, which once sprawled into several buildings in Columbus, couldn't hold out against the drain caused by urban crime and over-malling and was forced to shut its doors, which had been open since 1851.

The Rochester store was demolished after sitting vacant for a few years. The Great Oaks mall had not been particularly successful, and the loss of its only anchor was its death-knell. The whole complex was removed and replaced with a generic drugstore and a strip mall/office building combination of distinctly inferior architectural quality.

A similar process occurred in Florida, which had come to accept Jacobson's not as an outsider but as its own since 1969. The Naples store became a branch of Saks Fifth Avenue, while furniture stores moved into the Boca Raton and Altamonte locations. The Yankee Traveler, where Jacobson's

Florida story began, was subdivided into smaller tenant spaces, as were locations in Osprey, Tampa and Fort Myers. The Clearwater and North Palm Beach stores became Stein Mart discount stores, and the elaborate Jacksonville branch, attached to a failed shopping mall, has been converted into a community college.

Cities that had lost a Jacobson's store prior to the company's final disposition had a head start on finding a new tenant for the vacant buildings. It is an interesting commentary on the state of our cities that not a single downtown location houses a specialty or department store operation today, though the Ann Arbor store, which closed in 1992 with Jacobson's move to Briarwood, has housed the main store of Border's Books. Similarly, the East Lansing store is now in use as a Barnes & Noble Bookseller.

The exquisite Dearborn store was demolished and replaced with a residential complex featuring some ground-level shops. The famous bull was purchased by a collector and is happily existing outside in a poppy field on a farm in Chelsea, Michigan.

In Grosse Pointe, a series of proposals was put forth to replace the Williamsburg-style building with a midrise residential and retail development. The project fizzled amid objections by local residents, with the worsening economy driving the last nail in the coffin. The original building was reconfigured, and the parking deck at the rear was demolished and replaced with a larger facility. A drugstore and food market now exist where chic Grosse Pointers once bought designer items. The building's façade has been altered in a nondescript style, and very little about it hints at the splendor that reigned in the same location for thirty-eight years. The Store for the Home was once occupied by Border's as well, but that has since succumbed due to low traffic in the area. David McCarthy, a longtime area resident, says, "I can remember as a young man, in the '50s, seeing the line of limousines parked on Kercheval Avenue, with chauffeurs waiting for 'their ladies' to come out of Jacobson's. The liveried drivers either polished their cars or chatted among themselves while waiting. You won't ever see that again!"

Other Jacobson's stores, such as the Birmingham apparel store and the Kalamazoo store, have been rebuilt beyond recognition and house new office facilities. In Saginaw, an inner-city church proposed to occupy the ill-fated "superblock," but a lack of funding has stalled the project, and the building remains virtually empty and barricaded, surrounded by blight.

The Jackson store, the site of so much history described in this volume, has been transformed into a health clinic. In the process of re-cladding the building in contemporary materials, the black granite facing of the store's columns made its way into souvenir plaques that the contractor gave to friends who had been Jacobson's employees, and in one case, it was used to remodel a Jackson resident's kitchen!

The Esther Jacobson Building in Jackson still exists as well but has been clad with pink synthetic stucco. At the time of the building's dubious "renovation," the *Jackson Citizen-Patriot*, under a headline stating, "Sun Shines Again on City's Past," reminded Jackson citizens of the building's history. In the brief period between the removal of Jacobson's 1955 façade improvements and application of the stucco, the original carved letters, calling out "Jacobson's" and "Esther Jacobson Building," were momentarily visible before being covered up again.

It is hard to believe that the surrounding downtown, with its vacant storefronts, the forlorn Hotel Hayes and the brutally altered Albert-Kahn-designed Consumer's Power Building, was once a thriving retail center, serving to draw customers from as far away as Michigan's capital city, Lansing. The big downtown retail anchor, L.H. Field, sadly closed in 1987 and met with the wrecker's ball, replaced by a parking lot and a small office building bearing the merchant's name. Interestingly, during the demolition, removal of the 1950-era facing revealed the neo-Gothic splendor of the original building, but neither nostalgia for the store nor appreciation of its history were able to prevail against its destruction.

Perhaps customers' memories are one of the best ways to find Jacobson's in a post-Jacobson's era. While the preceding chapters have documented tales about them and their relationship with the store, opinions and attitudes about it are fairly consistent, even nine years after its demise. When planning a visit to a library for research, I was told by the librarian that she'd "wear something from good, old Jake's" to commemorate the store on the day of my visit. Likewise, the phrases "It's so sad that it's no longer here" or "I wish it could come back" are frequently uttered by those who knew the store, in the same manner as speaking about a departed friend. Accompanying these sentiments, former customers not only celebrate the friendliness and competence of the sales staff, but they also often remember the tiniest purchase made years ago in their favorite Jacobson's department as well.

Others from Jacobson's management have taken their experiences from mere memory into action. James Sontag spent twenty-five years working for Jacobson's, first in the East Lansing store and later as a buyer in the Jackson headquarters. He maintains a Facebook page for Jacobson's alumni, one of two currently on the Internet. "My years with the company are a testament to being satisfied in your career. There was such longevity among the employees; it was difficult for any retailer to lure a Jacobson's employee away from them. So difficult, in fact, after Jacobson's closed, I interviewed with the president of Saks, and he specifically asked me about it."

The profound truth of Jim's statement is illustrated by yet another anecdote about Nathan Rosenfeld. Disappointed that his friend Stanley Marcus's store took one of Jacobson's merchandise managers to Texas, he felt vindicated when Jacobson's was able to hire a top Neiman-Marcus salesperson. "We got the better end of that deal, I think" was his smug observation at the time.

Jim Sontag goes on to remark that "at least until the board dismissed Mark Rosenfeld, we were a company with tremendous heart. We were as fair to the people we bought our goods from as we were to our customers who bought the goods from us." He says, "It took some of us being forced out to realize just how good we had it!"

His experiences at Jacobson's, and his recollections of them, motivated him to create Zoëy Bloom, an accessory and gift shop in South Tampa with a strong Internet presence. The retailer's own press material sounds as if it could have been written for Jacobson's, extolling the virtues of merchandise uniqueness, avoidance of clichés and the store's policy of combing markets for interesting things, like "looking for a needle in a haystack." Another interesting Jacobson's connection is the display of merchandise in coordinated settings, as a customer would use them, again something promoted earlier at Jacobson's by Nathan Rosenfeld, especially in the older store's home furnishings displays.

On top of all that, Jim's partner is Jo Anne Rosenfeld, Mark Rosenfeld's wife. About their business, Mark Rosenfeld says, "I am an unpaid employee and bookkeeper, but I'll tell you, I've learned as much from Jim as he has from his experience at Jacobson's. By that I mean e-commerce. Remember, I left Jacobson's before the Internet became a factor in retail."

Other Jacobson's buyers have stayed closer to home. Patty Denton, herself a Jacobson's home furnishings buyer, operates the Lilac Tree, a charming home furnishings store on West Michigan Avenue in Jackson, which, on most days, appears to be a beehive of activity for the city's interior design community.

If the store itself isn't enough of an attraction, behind it is Café Lilla, a small bistro and coffee café that is the closest thing left to dining at one of Jacobson's well-regarded restaurants. While it features the "Garden Sandwich" on its menu, the real treasure is the Jacobson's cheese soup, which is offered on several days of the week. Café Lilla is another place in Jackson where simply mentioning the name Jacobson's will more often than not open the door to discussion about the store, because in the words of one of its employees, "most of us worked there."

June Johnson, a former salesperson in the Saginaw Coat and Suit Shop and described by Pam Schauffler as one of Jacobson's "legendary top performers," maintains her connection with Jacobson's and its people by organizing an annual reunion for Saginaw store alumni.

Creative employees, who were vital in executing the "Jacobson's style" in advertising, store design and display, have also found new niches. Larry Terrill, who worked under Keith Houck as corporate visual display coordinator and designed the store's famous black-and-white, scroll-pattern shopping bags, is a freelance cartoonist whose work can be seen in the Jackson Citizen-Patriot and Somerset [Pennsylvania] Daily American newspapers. Jackson store visual display manager Dick Stanton's pen-and-ink drawings can be admired at the Ella Sharp Museum's exhibits in conjunction with the Jackson Civic Art Association. Ted Matz—from 1987, Jacobson's corporate visual supervisor—worked for Saks Fifth Avenue in Florida for a time but has now retired and works as a fine artist and art instructor in the Sunshine State.

A trip into Jacobson's pre-Rosenfeld history can be made in Reed City, Michigan, where the original store building at 102 East Upton Avenue now houses a firm by the name of Pere Marquette Catering. Amid the building's original exposed brick walls, pressed metal ceiling, worn wood floors and an ancient safe in the corner, it operates a casual café serving light meals and is highly regarded by locals and visitors to the town, which Jacobson's called home in the distant, mostly forgotten past.

Perhaps the most surprising place to find Jacobson's in a world without Jacobson's is, in fact, Jacobson's. On Park Avenue, in Winter Park, Florida, in the same building as its predecessor (albeit altered beyond recognition), there exists a fashion retailer that uses the Jacobson's name and the familiar trademark as identifiers. Tammy Giaimo, the store's owner, decided to open a women's store after losing a close friend to brain cancer. "In contemplating what to call the store, the Jacobson's name quickly came to mind," she recalls. Giaimo purchased the name and trademark from bankruptcy court, and before long, a new Jacobson's was born. Unable to locate the store in the Proctor Center, which was undergoing redevelopment at the time, she attempted to replicate the Jacobson's format as much as available finances would allow. Giaimo explains her motivation by saying, "I felt that the departure of Jacobson's left a void in our community for a comfortable upscale retail experience. I loved the quality it represented and felt the name spoke volumes."

Finding Jacobson's

The first eleven-thousand-square-foot store opened in October 2004 but later downsized and moved back into the original Proctor Building on Park Avenue, where it continues to offer high-fashion names like Escada and St. John to discriminating Florida women, along with the personalized service and welcoming atmosphere that so characterized the store that inspired it.

Finally, remembrances of Jacobson's can be found in an excellent museum in its hometown of Jackson, Michigan. The Ella Sharp Museum of Art and History, south of downtown Jackson, was the recipient of Jacobson's store archives after it ceased to be. While specific items are held in the museum's vaults and are not accessible to the general public, the museum's exhibits, both permanent and temporary, do often allude to the store's influence on the city.

The Jackson History Gallery focuses on businesses and industries that called Jackson home. Jacobson's and Nathan Rosenfeld are among the "stars" of the gallery, but visitors to the museum can also see wonderful exhibits of period clothing (some from Jacobson's) and learn firsthand about little-known items like the Tom Thumb toy cash registers and typewriters that were Jackson-made products familiar to children in the 1950s and 1960s.

In fact, Nathan Rosenfeld, who liked to listen to anyone with an idea, was intrigued by the "no sale" key on a prototype toy cash register, shown to him by a local metal products company that needed Rosenfeld's support to bring the product to market. The story goes that the "no sale" key reminded him of a former boss who kept a full-size cash register in his office, and he discouragingly rang the "no sale" key whenever someone tried to pitch a new idea. With Rosenfeld's help, the toys went on to become a "ringing" success story, and Jackson had a slice of the toy market to add to its list of manufacturing industries.

The Ella Sharp Museum, located on a beautiful ten-acre estate donated for use as a museum and park by its namesake, also features art exhibits and a charming restaurant, Ella's Granary. Ella Sharp (1857–1912), a member of the Michigan Women's Hall of Fame since 1998, was an avid collector and world traveler. As a civic-minded person, she formed the Jackson Town Improvement Society, which was responsible for a great number of civic improvements, such as the first public drinking fountains, in Jackson. In this way, she paved the way for Nathan Rosenfeld's activities on behalf of his adopted hometown.

Seen in this light, the Ella Sharp Museum, which is entirely privately supported, is much more than a fitting resting place for the last vestiges of a store so well loved and sorely missed as Jacobson's.

Former Jacobson's employees: Top, from left to right, front row: Jan Curcio and Marikay Pigeon. Middle row: Janet Heatley, Carol Markesino, Sharon Vick, Elaine Coyne and Dolores Krosivek. Rear: Sandra Berardo. Bottom, from left to right: Sandra Meda, Lucille Howard, Linda Salah, Cheryl Kutscher, Cindy Brown and Sandy Berardo.

The Gifts of the Spirit

The policy of this business is predicated on the belief that no one has ever won an argument with a customer.
—Zola Rosenfeld

Among the many stories told about Jacobson's employees is this little gem. One Christmas Eve, a clearly distraught gentleman asked a saleslady at a cosmetics counter if she could help him select a present for his wife. "Perhaps you could tell me something about her," she said, "and we can go from there."

"Well," the customer replied, "she just ran away with my best friend."

Without hesitation, the saleslady answered, "Then I'd perhaps suggest a bottle of My Sin perfume by Lanvin!"

The salespeople who worked (and stayed, for the most part) at Jacobson's were the store's public face. Their skill, knowledge and willingness to accommodate were clearly fueled by a communal spirit that allowed them to do so with consummate grace. Possessed of this legendary spirit, they remain the most delightful remnant of Jacobson's, no matter whether they have taken other employment or have gone into retirement.

Regularly, groups of Jacobson's employees, who formed significant friendships and relationships during their tenures at the store, still get together on a regular basis to meet, talk about their experiences and keep up on their current exploits. In the course of these meetings, the conversation inevitably turns toward the amusing anecdotes and interesting descriptions of events they experienced while working for an employer they appreciated and respected.

Meeting at a restaurant, just blocks from the former Birmingham store, alumni from Jacobson's begin with the regular "hellos" and "how are yous," but in my presence, they chat about a world that has sadly passed. Elaine Coyne, the organizer of the group, mentions "the excellent alterations department Jacobson's always had. If we ripped a piece of our clothing, we could just walk in there, and they'd fix it on the spot. They were exceptionally good. It was an inside joke—we called it the 'International Room' because they were Poles, Czechs and Italians, always chattering away in their own languages!" (The International Collection was the name of one of Jacobson's in-store shops.)

One of her colleagues, Dolores Krosivek, who worked in sportswear, soon interjects, "Do you remember that one crusty old saleslady we had? What was her name? You know, the one who would ask people why they were returning an item, and if they said, 'I don't like it,' she'd say sarcastically, 'Well, ya liked it two weeks ago!' That wasn't the kind of thing a Jacobson's salesperson should have said!"

In a less boisterous tone, Sharon Vick remembers the seasonal fashion previews that employees could attend in Jackson. "Each season, a bus would pick us up and take us there for a lovely show previewing the upcoming season's fashions. They always had a beautiful spread of food laid out for us, and they even gave us a goodie bag at the end, just like celebrities get at an awards show. It was more than just a good time because it helped us in our jobs, and it made us feel so valued to be included in an important event like that."

Others, like Jan Curcio, Carol Markesino, Marikay Pigeon and Janet Heatley, agree and throw out story after interesting story about the daily lives of employees working behind the scenes at this most refined of stores. "Do you remember" is how most of the tales begin, and they cover topics from the store's many events for children to its customer appreciation parties, where, after store hours, the best customers were shuttled around downtown Birmingham in horse-drawn carriages. Even an animal-loving employee is recalled, one who tried to keep an abandoned chick, found on her lunch hour, in her locker until it could be taken home!

Unequivocally, they talk about what they call "fun times" at their jobs. One of them pipes in to add that if a saleswoman, on her feet for many hours, had a moment to slip off her shoes, she had better watch out, not for the reprimand of a manager, but because one of her co-workers would, more often than not, hide them on her as a prank.

The Gifts of the Spirit

Sandy Berardo, who worked in Grosse Pointe for twenty eight years, regularly organizes a group from the store that was for so long a familiar landmark on Kercheval Avenue. They speak animatedly about "Mrs. Pete" and how Jacobson's "gros-grain ribbons, which were a part of the complimentary gift wrapping, were of the finest quality." Sandy herself makes a point of saying that Jacobson's employees worked hard, but she mostly recalls the enjoyment of working for the company. "It was like being in a big, warm family" is how she sums up her years at Jacobson's.

Indeed, their stories bear this out and offer valuable insight into just what it was like to serve the Jacobson's customer. Linda Salah, whose thirty years at Jacobson's saw her go from salesperson to human resources manager to operations manager in Grosse Pointe and Great Oaks, remembers out loud that there was very little that the salespeople wouldn't do for "their" customers.

She asks Sandy, "Do you want to tell the story about the dishes or should I?" They take turns explaining how a customer called to say that the set of dishes she bought at Jacobson's wouldn't clean properly, and she wanted someone to come and pick them up. "It was a dark, snowy evening after we closed, and we must have asked every utility worker in the area how to find her house, which was in an out-of-the-way location. To top it off, we had our high heels on from work and had to walk through several inches of snow up to this house, which seemed inordinately dark." Linda picks up the story, saying, "We got to the door, and when the woman opened it, we noticed that the house was pitch dark inside. 'We're here from Jacobson's to pick up the dishes,' I said, and she let us in. So there we were, feeling around walls in the dark, in order to follow her to the kitchen, and I asked, 'Just where are they?' 'Oh,' she said, 'they're in the cupboard.' So I finally got her to turn on a light, and when I found them, I could see that they had never been washed, just stacked and put away dirty."

Sandy Berardo gets to the point. "That's when we realized she was blind. Since we thought that the dishes would be packed in their original box, all we had was one lone Jake's bag in the car. So we made trips back and forth through the snow, filling the bag and carrying the dishes out to the trunk of the car and back again until we had it all."

The moral of the story becomes apparent when Linda brings it to a conclusion. "Through all of this, I never thought to do anything but ask her how she wanted us to credit the price of the dishes. That's what we were trained to do; that's what Jacobson's meant by customer service."

Linda's cousin, Lucille Howard, who also worked at the Grosse Pointe store, adds, "You will never find a store like Jacobson's. Never, ever again.

The only way you would is if we all got together again and opened it back up, to show these stores today what 'customer service' really means. In fact, I'd say that we never really felt like Jacobson's employees; we actually believed that this was our company, so we took ownership of whatever we did."

Linda adds a story about a time she answered the phone in the Grosse Pointe store and a caller asked about the hours of the Edsel and Eleanor Ford House Museum in Grosse Pointe Shores. "Now, since I had just been there, I knew what the hours were, so I told her," she says. "But I asked her if she knew that she called Jacobson's. She said yes but continued to ask about the address and then again about their Sunday hours. I finally questioned her as to why she called us, and she answered that she figured Jacobson's would know just about anything!"

Sandra Meda, a twenty-one-year Jacobson's veteran, chimes in with further insight into Jacobson's customer service, but from a different standpoint: "We had something called the eleven o'clock club. These were the top salespeople, who had all of the best customers. They took lunch at eleven, because they wanted to be on the floor at lunchtime when their customers usually came in. In fact, you really couldn't join them at the table even; that's how exclusive they were."

She explains that all Jacobson's salespeople had a "P.T. (Personal Trade) Book" in which they recorded information about their customers so that they knew their likes and dislikes. Using this information, they could send greeting cards on important dates or contact them when new merchandise came in, thereby forming a strong relationship with individual customers. She gives an example of how this practice could be put into use by recalling Mrs. DeWitt, a beautiful Grosse Pointe socialite whose family's nationally known seed company was headquartered in Detroit.

"She called one day and said that she had to go to Japan for some reason and told her favorite saleslady that she dreaded packing for the trip." With a smile, Sandra adds that "she asked the salesgirl if she could go to the luggage department, pick out some bags and fill them with whatever she might need for the trip—clothing, shoes, hosiery, even cosmetics. And by the way, could Jacobson's deliver them to the airport next Tuesday before her flight leaves?" She continues, "It wasn't as though that was anything out of the ordinary. That particular gal (a member of the eleven o'clock club) was accustomed to serving Mrs. Ford, the Dodges and a lot of other famous people. You name them, she had them! And we all knew that there wasn't anything one of these customers would be denied. We were trained that there was really nothing *but* customer service at Jacobson's."

The Gifts of the Spirit

To put the icing on the cake, Sandra goes on to relate that Mrs. DeWitt's luggage, full of Jacobson's merchandise, was indeed delivered to the airport as requested, but the airline lost it in transit, leaving her stranded in Japan without a single thing. When the airline asked her to describe it, in order to make a claim, she was forced to call Jacobson's, which dutifully relayed the sales slips to the airline's lost luggage bureau, half a globe away.

Cheryl Kutscher, whose eight years with the store seems short by comparison, says, "Do you know what I loved most of all? It was what I call 'The Art of Selling.' Take, for instance, hosiery. You didn't just grab it from a rack. It was kept in boxes, in little drawers behind a counter. The saleslady would take it out, and put her hand inside to show the color. The same thing was true of gloves. If you wanted a pair of white kid gloves, you had to try on a dark pair for size first. That way, no one ever purchased a soiled pair of white gloves. And the salespeople were highly specialized; they really knew their gloves, hosiery or whatever they sold." She adds that her second favorite thing was Jacobson's fashion shows, which she classes as "phenomenal." "I remember when Oscar de la Renta came in for a runway show and, afterward, thanked everyone involved personally. He had such grace and dignity. I was probably eighteen at the time, and it made a real impression upon me."

She adds a humorous story about a woman who had a habit of returning her brassieres to the store when she had wore them out. Jacobson's customarily accepted the return, but the salespeople, when seeing that her house had been renovated with a completely new front, referred to it as "the house the bras built." In fact, there was a humorous quip, circulated among salespeople in Grosse Pointe, that a customer "only really had to buy a wardrobe once" because of the store's liberal return policy.

Cindy Brown is an alumni of Jacobson's who can look back on twenty-seven years with the company, working in Battle Creek, Kalamazoo and Grosse Pointe. In the middle of all this, she served as a home furnishings buyer in the Jackson headquarters. While she admits that there was some stratification of employees at central distribution, she is proud of the close rapport between the buyers and the staff who worked in the stores. The salespeople were eager to call and order more merchandise because they knew what they could and could not sell. From her days in the store, she likes to remember that people often came in for wedding gifts between a morning church ceremony and the reception later in the day. "They just knew we'd have what they wanted, and it would get wrapped up, so they could be on their way with a minimum of effort."

She reminds her friends that she once asked Marjorie Rosenfeld, who was making a purchase, what her discount at Jacobson's was. The owner's wife replied, "Why, it's the same as everybody else." In fact, it was policy under the Rosenfeld's ownership of Jacobson's that no executive got any better discount than the rest of Jacobson's employees, no matter who they were.

The employees talk about the wonderful food and hospitality in the St. Clair Room and about the store's many special events, such as the legendary pre-Christmas Men's Nights, magic shows for children, the traditional Breakfast with Santa or the local Thanksgiving Day parade, when Santa Claus arrived at Jacobson's. "That's when I knew it was Christmas," Sandy Berardo says. "When I heard all of those kids screaming and applauding atop the stairs, which were near the store offices on the lower level where I worked."

There are sad memories as well. The employees talk about how they strove to give the same type of service during the liquidation period as when the store was going strong, in "the good old days." They talk about how the liquidators, whose job it was to shut down retailers across the country, couldn't believe how clean and orderly the store was kept in its last days or that after the close of business on any particular day, salespeople stayed to tidy up their areas and restock and colorize merchandise on the shelves and racks. "It was still Jacobson's to us," one of them proclaims.

They are in general agreement that things changed "when the new group came in and tried to tell us how to do our jobs." They saw a deterioration in their relationship with management and also in the store's clientele. Through it all, though, they "never really thought it would close…until the writing was on the wall."

Linda Salah, who keeps the date of Jacobson's bankruptcy filing and final closure marked in her pocket calendar every year, says, "I was the last person to lock the door at the last store on the last day that Jacobson's was in business. I don't mind telling you that I cried when I turned the key. I looked in one last time and it was as if all of those beautiful counters and bins were calling to me, saying, 'How could this happen, where is everybody?'" Thinking back to her years as operations manager at Great Oaks, she offers a last insight into the relationship between the company and its employees.

"We had a longtime employee at the Great Oaks store named Hazel Pill. She worked until well into her eighties, still wearing heels and dressing to the nines every day for work. Her regular customers adored her, and she was the type of person who would just love you to death. By the time she was eighty-six, she had slowed down a little, but in our eyes she was still exemplary. One day a man, whom she had served, came to me and said, 'That woman has no business working in this store at her age.' When he persisted and said she should be let go, I had no problem telling him that it just wasn't going to happen. I let him know that we care about our employees, and as long as she wants to work, she could." With a grin, she adds, "From the Jacobson's standpoint, I didn't feel I was acting out of line by suggesting he was the one we didn't need as a customer. We were truly a family, and that's how we operated."

It doesn't take long to realize that, in a deeply spiritual way, Jacobson's still exists in the hearts, minds and memories of these, or any of the other extraordinary people referenced in these pages. Their experience as the human representatives of a great institution put them in front of the public, which the store served so well. That they did so with the grace and hospitality as required by Nathan Rosenfeld and his ideals is unquestionable, even years after the store's demise.

Though it is irretrievably gone, it is the fond remembrance of Jacobson's that keeps it alive in a way. The sense of retrospection is perhaps best illustrated by one of these employees, who, when asked to give an overall opinion of Jacobson's, leaned in close, focused her gaze and said, "It was friggin' awesome is what it was!"

Appendix A

Jacobson's Timeline

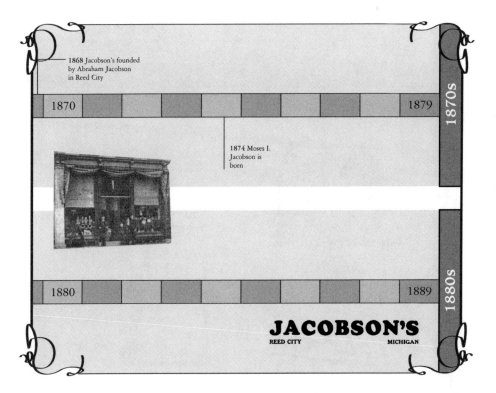

1868 Jacobson's founded
by Abraham Jacobson
in Reed City

1870   1879   1870s

1874 Moses I.
Jacobson is
born

1880   1889   1880s

JACOBSON'S
REED CITY   MICHIGAN

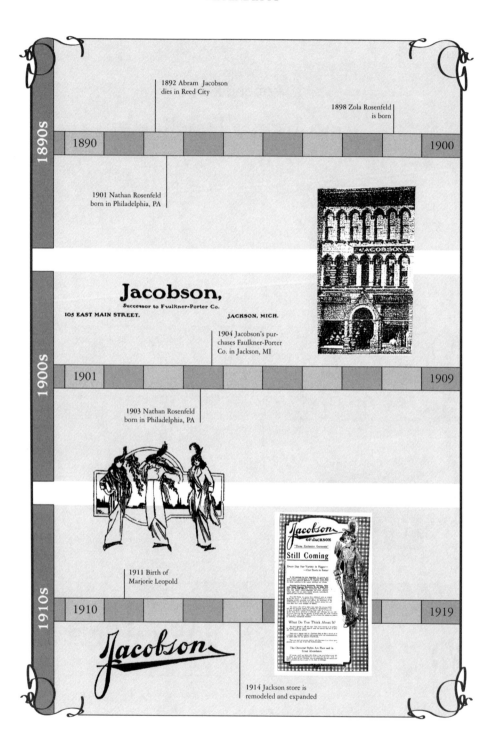

1892 Abram Jacobson
dies in Reed City

1898 Zola Rosenfeld
is born

1890s

1890   1900

1901 Nathan Rosenfeld
born in Philadelphia, PA

Jacobson,
Successor to Faulkner-Porter Co.
105 EAST MAIN STREET.   JACKSON, MICH.

1904 Jacobson's pur-
chases Faulkner-Porter
Co. in Jackson, MI

1900s

1901   1909

1903 Nathan Rosenfeld
born in Philadelphia, PA

1911 Birth of
Marjorie Leopold

1910s

1910   1919

1914 Jackson store is
remodeled and expanded

Jacobson's Timeline

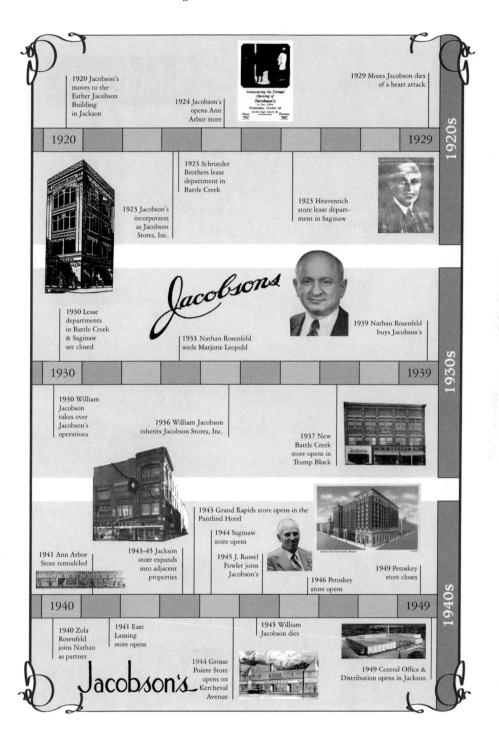

1920 Jacobson's moves to the Esther Jacobson Building in Jackson

1924 Jacobson's opens Ann Arbor store

1929 Moses Jacobson dies of a heart attack

1920   **1929**

1923 Schroeder Brothers lease department in Battle Creek

1923 Jacobson's incorporates as Jacobson Stores, Inc.

1923 Heavenrich store lease department in Saginaw

1930 Lease departments in Battle Creek & Saginaw are closed

1933 Nathan Rosenfeld weds Marjorie Leopold

1939 Nathan Rosenfeld buys Jacobson's

1930   **1939**

1930 William Jacobson takes over Jacobson's operations

1936 William Jacobson inherits Jacobson Stores, Inc.

1937 New Battle Creek store opens in Trump Block

1943 Grand Rapids store opens in the Pantlind Hotel

1944 Saginaw store opens

1941 Ann Arbor Store remodeled

1943-45 Jackson store expands into adjacent properties

1945 J. Russel Fowler joins Jacobson's

1946 Petoskey store opens

1949 Petoskey store closes

1940   **1949**

1940 Zola Rosenfeld joins Nathan as partner

1941 East Lansing store opens

1945 William Jacobson dies

1944 Grosse Pointe Store opens on Kercheval Avenue

1949 Central Office & Distribution opens in Jackson

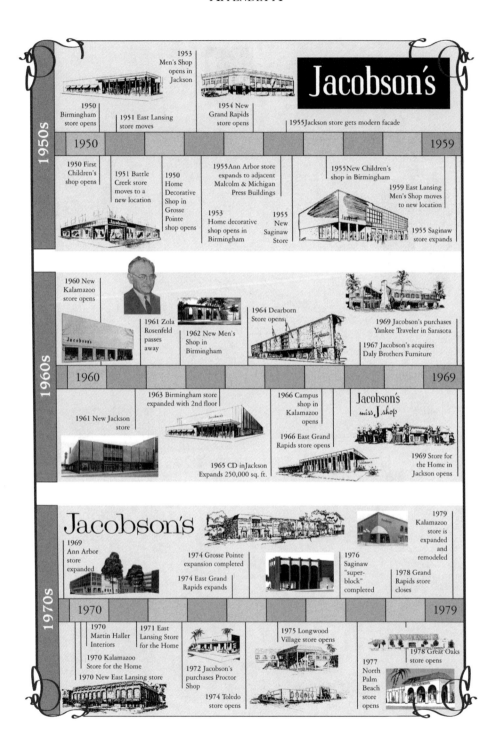

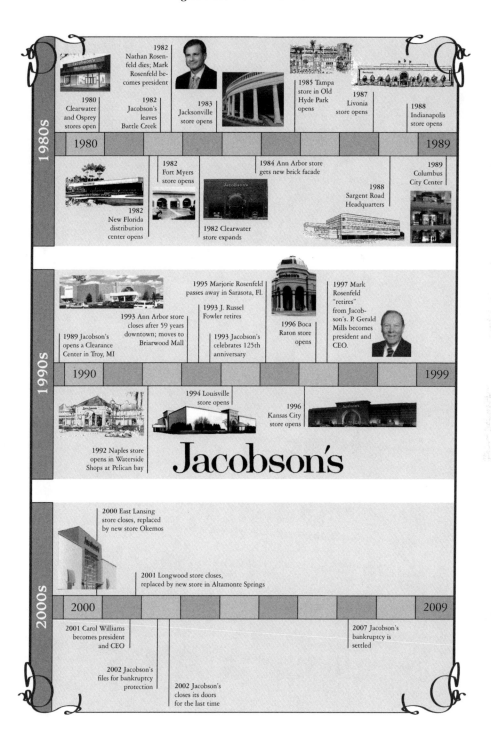

1980s

1980 Clearwater and Osprey stores open

1982 Jacobson's leaves Battle Creek

1982 Nathan Rosenfeld dies; Mark Rosenfeld becomes president

1983 Jacksonville store opens

1985 Tampa store in Old Hyde Park opens

1987 Livonia store opens

1988 Indianapolis store opens

1980

1989

1982 New Florida distribution center opens

1982 Fort Myers store opens

1982 Clearwater store expands

1984 Ann Arbor store gets new brick facade

1988 Sargent Road Headquarters

1989 Columbus City Center

1990s

1989 Jacobson's opens a Clearance Center in Troy, MI

1993 Ann Arbor store closes after 59 years downtown; moves to Briarwood Mall

1993 J. Russel Fowler retires

1993 Jacobson's celebrates 125th anniversary

1995 Marjorie Rosenfeld passes away in Sarasota, Fl.

1996 Boca Raton store opens

1997 Mark Rosenfeld "retires" from Jacobson's. P. Gerald Mills becomes president and CEO.

1990

1999

1992 Naples store opens in Waterside Shops at Pelican bay

1994 Louisville store opens

1996 Kansas City store opens

Jacobson's

2000s

2000 East Lansing store closes, replaced by new store Okemos

2001 Longwood store closes, replaced by new store in Altamonte Springs

2000

2009

2001 Carol Williams becomes president and CEO

2002 Jacobson's files for bankruptcy protection

2002 Jacobson's closes its doors for the last time

2007 Jacobson's bankruptcy is settled

Jacobson's Store Locations

MICHIGAN AND TOLEDO, OHIO

Jackson	#010	(1904)
Ann Arbor	#020	(1924)
Battle Creek	#030	(1937)
East Lansing	#040	(1942)
Grand Rapids	#050	(1943)
Saginaw	#060	(1944)
Grosse Pointe	#070	(1944)
Petoskey		(1946–1949)
Birmingham	#080	(1950)
Kalamazoo	#090	(1960)
Dearborn	#100	(1964)
East Grand Rapids	#051	(1966)
Toledo	#200	(1974)
Rochester	#120	(1978)
Livonia	#130	(1987)

Appendix B

Florida

Sarasota	#310	(1969)
Winter Park	#320	(1972)
Longwood	#330	(1975)
North Palm Beach	#340	(1977)
Osprey	#350	(1980)
Clearwater	#360	(1980)
Jacksonville	#370	(1982)
Ft. Myers	#380	(1982)
Tampa	#410	(1985)
Naples	#420	(1992)
Boca Raton	#430	(1996)

Midwest

Indianapolis	#510	(1988)
Columbus	#210	(1989)
Louisville	#520	(1994)
Kansas City	#530	(1996)

NOTE:
Short-lived stores were opened in Okemos, Michigan in 2000 and Altamonte Springs, Florida in 2002.

Appendix C

Nathanisms

I wish I had met Mrs. Rosenfeld sooner because she's been a wonderful person to live with.

I believe that everyone, even if he is an atheist, needs a day for a little bit of introspection.

I think the greatest penalty that we can impose on someone is to make them feel that they don't have to work.

I wanted to build an organization for two reasons: that's the way you build a business, and that's the only way a business survives.

We have two responsibilities. A social responsibility and a responsibility to run the business profitably.

There's a great future in retailing for those of us who give our business a certain personality.

We just opened a store in a mall, and they had to meet our standards or we would not have gone in there. Among other things, the stores in there will not be allowed to use gimmicks, store prizes, doorbusters or premiums of any kind. We just don't believe in that.

The experts said that the children's wear business would become unimportant. We felt that if families were smaller, the people would spend as much to take care of two children as they can spend to take care of four.

When I first came to Michigan, I'd drive into Detroit around four thirty in the afternoon when the men were coming out of the automobile plants—the first shift—and you'd see a man that looked as though he was fifty-five or sixty; he'd have a pouch from drinking too much beer, and he might be only thirty. Unless we take care of ourselves, we all go to pot. And if we have a business, and we don't take care of it…if all we're doing is trying to get immediate profit, and don't think ahead…then our business goes to pot.

We're very proud that 98 percent of Jacobson's volume represents the development of a great idea, and only 2 percent by acquisition. The great idea is to take something small that's worthwhile and build it up by working hard at it rather than the idea of buying other companies to make your business big.

Years ago, in the average department store, you'd see all the sofas together, the chairs, beds, tables. Jacobson's was one of the first to arrange merchandise functionally, the way people use it, in room settings.

The biggest changes that have taken place in retailing since I started? The biggest investment a retailer needs today is a magnificent plant. Secondly, accounts receivable because more and more people are using credit. Third, an adequate inventory because people want selection.

We insist that our buyers sell things without the slightest bit of exaggeration. We force them to try their hardest to buy the best values that people recognize as value.

We start out with the premise that we're not as smart as the customers. Whenever the customer decides that the item is not worth what we're asking, we mark it down because the customer is boss. They know more about it than we do.

No designer or manufacturer is so important to us that we will ever violate our principle of buying to fit the needs of our customers.

Nathanisms

When we make a mistake, we take the markdown, but the reason we don't budget the markdowns is you can't budget mistakes. When they happen, they happen. We know we're going to make mistakes, particularly if we buy high-style things where the risk is great. Even the designer can't predict whether or not the style will be accepted.

I think women look their best when they are interested in being proud of the way they look. There are some people, especially young people, who look so sloppy that they can't possibly look good because they have no pride in the way they look.

People need help in being presentable. If you pick the wrong size for yourself, or if you don't have a well-informed salesperson to tell you all about the product, you may end up wasting your money.

Even those of us who are reasonably successful always feel that we are not as successful as we'd hope to be.

Consumer credit should be used to benefit the consumer and not the retailer who tries to make his profit on finance charges.

We have a certain amount of self-selection with good salespeople to help the customer. But if you only sell things that people can pick off the shelf in a package and satisfy the demand created by the manufacturer with his tremendous advertising budget, before long retailers become nothing more than big vending machines with checkout counters.

Departments and Directories

J acobson's differed somewhat from many other department stores in terms of its advertising, which was very classic and understated. The store, while it did have specific names for many of its varied shops and departments, generally did not identify these departments in print advertising, with a few notable exceptions, such as the Miss J Shop and Mr. J Shop, which were characterized by their own logos. The following store directories are presented in order to give an idea how typical Jacobson's stores were arranged and the names carried by Jacobson's various shops and departments.

It is necessary to bear in mind that the complex histories of the stores themselves, and the company in general, makes it difficult to pinpoint this type of data at a certain time. The directories reflect the individual stores during the mid- to late 1970s. Changes often occurred as stores were expanded and remodeled. To illustrate, the famous and well-remembered Miss J Shop began as a Campus Shop in Ann Arbor and was renamed the Young Timers Shop in 1961 before the first Miss J Shop was developed later in the 1960s. In time, it became Ms. J and ultimately Che Bella! The Mr. J Shop was first known as the Quad Shop.

The stores also differed in their offerings by community. Some had special designer boutiques such as St. Laurent/Rive Gauche and Givenchy Nouvelle Boutique. Interestingly, Jacobson's sold sewing fabrics and needlework supplies, but only at selected locations. The varying sizes of the stores meant that some departments were not located in all stores. The Florida stores varied greatly in size, and this was reflected in their merchandise mix as well.

JACKSON

255 West Michigan Avenue • *783-2841*

STREET FLOOR
Stationery • Adult Game Gallery • Pantry and Sweet Shop • Luggage • Fine Jewelry Salon • Cosmetics • Jewelry • Handbags • Small Leather Goods • Gloves • Belts • Scarves • Accessories • Little Separates • Hosiery • Lingerie • Patio Fashions • Shoe Salon • Offices
Men's Store Men's Furnishings • Men's Sportswear • Mr. J Shop • Men's Clothing • Men's Shoes
Cortland Street Cortland Room Restaurant (First Floor) • Styling Salon

SECOND FLOOR
Maternity Wear • Sportswear • Pin Money Shop • Custom Sizes • Dresses • Coats and Suits • After 5 Dresses • Young Signature Collections • International Collections • Collection Sportswear • Designer Salon • Bridal Salon • Fur Salon
Children's Shops Infants' Shop • Boys' Shop • Cannon Shop • Girls' Shop • Teens Shop • Toys • Children's Shoes

THIRD FLOOR
Miss J Shop • Miss J Shoes

STORE FOR THE HOME
270 West Cortland Street

Dining Center China • Silver • Glass • Linen Shop
Bath & Boudoir Shop Bedroom Fashions • Bath Shop • Carlin Shop
Gifts for the Home • Kitchen Shop • Curtains and Draperies • Closet Shop • Fine Furniture Galleria • Collector's Gallery • Interior Design Studio • Lamps • Pictures and Mirrors • Floor Coverings • Area Rug Center • Sleep Shop

Departments and Directories

ANN ARBOR

612 East Liberty Street • *769-7600*

LOWER LEVEL
Stationery • Adult Game Gallery • Pantry and Sweet Shop • Toys • Offices
Dining Center China • Silver • Glass • Linen Shop
Bath & Boudoir Shop Bedroom Fashions • Bath Shop • Mowbray Shop
Gifts for the Home • Kitchen Shop • Curtains and Draperies • Closet Shop •
Fine Furniture Galleria • Collector's Gallery • Collector's Gallery • Interior
Design Studio • Lamps • Pictures and Mirrors • Floor Coverings • Area Rug
Center • Sleep Shop

STREET FLOOR
Fine Jewelry Salon • Cosmetics • Jewelry • Handbags • Small Leather
Goods • Gloves • Belts • Luggage • Scarves • Accessories • Little Separates
• Hosiery • Lingerie • Patio Fashions • Shoe Salon • Miss J Shop • Miss
J Shoes
Men's Store Men's Furnishings • Men's Sportswear • Men's Clothing •
Men's Shoes

312–314 STATE STREET
Mr. J Shop

SECOND FLOOR
Sportswear • Pin Money Shop • Custom Sizes • Dresses • Coats and Suits
• After 5 Dresses • Young Signature Collections • International Collections
• Givenchy Nouvelle Boutique • Collection Sportswear • Designer Salon •
Bridal Salon • Fur Salon • Pappagallo Shop • Styling Salon
Children's Shops Infants' Shop • Children's Shop • Boys' Shop • Cannon Shop
• Girls' Shop • Teens Shop • Children's Shoes

APPENDIX D

GROSSE POINTE

17030 Kercheval Avenue • *882-7000*

LOWER LEVEL
Miss J Shop • Miss J Shoes • Offices

STREET FLOOR
Stationery • Adult Game Gallery • Pantry and Sweet Shop • Luggage • Fine Jewelry Salon • St. Clair Room Restaurant • Cosmetics • Jewelry • Handbags • Small Leather Goods • Gloves • Belts • Scarves • Accessories • Hosiery • Shoe Salon • Pappagallo Shop • Millinery
Men's Store Men's Furnishings • Men's Sportswear • Mr. J Shop • Men's Clothing • Men's Shoes

SECOND FLOOR
Children's Shops Infants' Shop • Boys' Shop • Cannon Shop • Girls' Shop • Teens Shop • Toys • Children's Shoes
Lingerie • Patio Fashions • Maternity Wear • Sportswear • Little Separates • Pin Money Shop • Custom Sizes • Dresses • Coats and Suits • After 5 Dresses • Young Signature Collections • International Collections • Givenchy Nouvelle Boutique • Collection Sportswear • Designer Salon • Bridal Salon • Fur Salon • Styling Salon

FABRIC SHOP
17015 Kercheval
Fabric Shop • Yarn Shop

STORE FOR THE HOME
17141 Kercheval Avenue

Dining Center China • Silver • Glass • Linen Shop
Bath & Boudoir Shop Bedroom Fashions • Bath Shop • Carlin Shop
Gifts for the Home • Kitchen Shop • Lamps • Pictures and Mirrors • Curtains & Draperies • Closet Shop • Fine Furniture Galleria • Collector's Gallery • Interior Design Studio • Floor Coverings • Area Rug Center • Sleep Shop

Departments and Directories

BIRMINGHAM

Apparel Store 336 West Maple Road • *644-6900*

LOWER LEVEL
Offices • Styling Salon

STREET LEVEL
Stationery • Adult Game Gallery • Pantry and Sweet Shop • Luggage • Fine Jewelry Salon • Cosmetics • Jewelry • Handbags • Small Leather Goods • Gloves • Belts • Scarves • Accessories • Hosiery

SECOND FLOOR
Lingerie • Patio Fashions • Maternity Wear • Sportswear • Little Separates • Pin Money Shop • Custom Sizes • Dresses • Coats and Suits • After 5 Dresses • Young Signature Collections • International Collections • Givenchy Nouvelle Boutique • YSL/Rive Gauche • Collection Sportswear • Designer Salon • Bridal Salon • Fur Salon • Shoe Salon • Pappagallo Shop • Millinery

CHILDREN'S SHOPS
275 North Woodward
Infants' Shop • Boys' Shop • Cannon Shop • Girls' Shop • Teens Shop • Toys • Children's Shoes

MEN'S STORE AND STORE FOR THE HOME
325 North Woodward

STREET FLOOR
Men's Store Men's Furnishings • Men's Sportswear • Mr. J Shop • Men's Clothing • Men's Shoes
Dining Center China • Silver • Glass • Linen Shop
Bath & Boudoir Shop Bedroom Fashions • Bath Shop • Carlin Shop
Gifts for the Home • Kitchen Shop • Curtains and Draperies • Closet Shop • Yarn Shop

UPPER LEVEL
Fine Furniture Galleria • Collector's Gallery • Interior Design Studio • Floor Coverings • Area Rug Center • Sleep Shop • Lamps • Pictures and Mirrors

Appendix D

Dearborn

22201 West Michigan Avenue • *565-9500*

Lower Level
Kitchen Shop • Curtains and Draperies • Closet Shop • Fabric Shop • Yarn Shop
Bath & Boudoir Shop Bedroom Fashions • Bath Shop • Carlin Shop

Street Floor
Stationery • Adult Game Gallery • Sweets and Treats Shop • Fine Jewelry Salon • Cosmetics • Jewelry • Handbags • Small Leather Goods • Gloves • Belts • Scarves • Accessories • Little Separates • Hosiery • Shoe Salon • Pappagallo Shop • Luggage
Dining Center China • Silver • Glass • Linen Shop • Gift Shop
Men's Store Men's Furnishings • Men's Sportswear • Mr. J Shop • Cannon Shop • Men's Clothing • Men's Shoes

Second Floor
Top of the Fountain Restaurant • Styling Salon • Miss J Shop • Miss J Shoes • Lingerie • Patio Fashions • Maternity Wear • Sportswear • Little Separates • Pin Money Shop • Custom Sizes • Dresses • Coats and Suits • After 5 Dresses • Signature Collections • International Collections • Collection Sportswear • Designer Salon • Bridal Salon • Fur Salon • Offices
Children's Shops Infants' Shop • Boys' Shop • Cannon Shop • Girls' Shop • Teens Shop • Toys • Children's Shoes

Store for the Home
22375 West Michigan Avenue

Fine Furniture Gallery • Interior Design Studio • Floor Coverings • Area Rug Center • Sleep Shop • Lamps • Pictures and Mirrors • Collector's Gallery

Departments and Directories

East Lansing

333 East Grand River Avenue • *351-2550*

LOWER LEVEL
Miss J Shop • Miss J Shoes • Mr. J Shop
Dining Center China • Silver • Glass • Linen Shop
Bath & Boudoir Shop Bedroom Fashions • Bath Shop • Carlin Shop
Gifts for the Home • Kitchen Shop • Lamps

STREET FLOOR
Stationery • Adult Game Gallery • Sweets and Treats Shop • Fine Jewelry
Salon • Cosmetics • Jewelry • Handbags • Small Leather Goods • Gloves
• Belts • Scarves • Accessories • Little Separates • Hosiery • Shoe Salon •
Pappagallo Shop • Intimate Apparel • Foundations • Patio Fashions
Men's Store Men's Furnishings • Men's Sportswear • Cannon Shop • Men's
Clothing • Men's Shoes

SECOND FLOOR
Maternity Wear • Sportswear • Little Separates • Pin Money Shop • Custom
Sizes • Dresses • Coats and Suits • After 5 Dresses • Signature Collections •
International Collections • Collection Sportswear • Designer Salon • Bridal
Salon • Fur Salon • Styling Salon

THIRD FLOOR
East Room Restaurant • Offices
Children's Shops Infants' Shop • Children's Shop • Boys' Shop • Girls' Shop •
Toys • Children's Shoes

STORE FOR THE HOME
115 East Grand River

STREET FLOOR
Fine Furniture Gallery • Interior Design Studio • Floor Coverings • Area
Rug Center • Lamps • Pictures and Mirrors • Collector's Gallery

LOWER LEVEL
Sleep Shop • Fine Furniture Gallery

APPENDIX D

TOLEDO

Franklin Park Mall

STREET FLOOR
Stationery • Adult Game Gallery • Sweets and Treats Shop • Fine Jewelry Salon • Cosmetics • Jewelry • Handbags • Small Leather Goods • Gloves • Belts • Scarves • Accessories • Little Separates • Hosiery • Shoe Salon • Pappagallo Shop • Intimate Apparel • Foundations • Patio Fashions • Miss J Shop • Miss J Shoes • Maternity Wear • Sportswear • Little Separates • Pin Money Shop • Custom Sizes • Dresses • Coats and Suits • After 5 Dresses • Young Signature Collections • International Collections • Collection Sportswear • Designer Salon • Bridal Salon • Fur Salon
Children's Shops Infants' Shop • Children's Shop • Boys' Shop • Girls' Shop • Toys • Children's Shoes
Men's Store Men's Furnishings • Men's Sportswear • Mr. J Shop • Cannon Shop • Men's Clothing • Men's Shoes

SECOND FLOOR
Dining Center China • Silver • Glass • Linen Shop
Bath & Boudoir Shop Bedroom Fashions • Bath Shop • Carlin Shop
Gifts for the Home • Kitchen Shop • Lamps • Fine Furniture Gallery • Collector's Gallery • Design Studio • Floor Coverings • Area Rug Center • Lamps • Pictures and Mirrors • Collector's Gallery • Sleep Shop • Offices • Styling Salon

Jacobson's "Million Dollar Round Table emblem. *Courtesy of Mark Rosenfeld.*

About the Author

Bruce Allen Kopytek was born in Hamtramck, Michigan, into a very inquisitive Polish-American family, who, despite their working-class bearing, valued faith, education and culture above everything else. As a result, he traveled widely as a youth and still does today with his wife, Carole. They reside in Shelby Township, where he practices architecture, a field in which he has over thirty-two years of experience, having designed various commercial and residential projects locally, nationally and abroad. A music enthusiast, book collector, history buff and avid ballroom dancer, Bruce also participates in pastoral work at his home parish, St. Lawrence, in Utica, Michigan. Bruce maintains a blog entitled "The Department Store Museum" and, when not home, is most likely poking around some very old place in Europe. At home, he is most likely being chased and bitten by a wild pussycat named Bella.

Visit us at
www.historypress.net